Smiling and Laughter across Contexts and the Life-span (SmiLa2022)

Held at LREC 2022

Marseille, France
24 June 2022

Editors:

Chiara Mazzocconi
Kevin El Haddad
Catherine Pelachaud
Gary McKeown

ISBN: 978-1-7138-6140-9

Printed from e-media with permission by:

Curran Associates, Inc.
57 Morehouse Lane
Red Hook, NY 12571

Some format issues inherent in the e-media version may also appear in this print version.

Printed with permission by Curran Associates, Inc. (2023)

For permission requests, please contact the Association for Computational Linguistics at the address below.

Association for Computational Linguistics
209 N. Eighth Street
Stroudsburg, Pennsylvania 18360

Phone: 1-570-476-8006
Fax: 1-570-476-0860

acl@aclweb.org

Additional copies of this publication are available from:

Curran Associates, Inc.
57 Morehouse Lane
Red Hook, NY 12571 USA
Phone: 845-758-0400
Fax: 845-758-2633
Email: curran@proceedings.com
Web: www.proceedings.com

LREC 2022 Workshop
Language Resources and Evaluation Conference
20-25 June 2022

Smiling and Laughter across Contexts and the Life-span (SmiLa2022)

PROCEEDINGS

Editors:
Chiara Mazzocconi
Kevin El Haddad
Catherine Pelachaud
Gary McKeown

Proceedings of the LREC 2022 workshop on Smiling and Laughter across Contexts and the Life-span (SmiLa 2022)

Edited by:
Chiara Mazzocconi, Kevin El Haddad, Catherine Pelachaud, Gary McKeown

For more information:
European Language Resources Association (ELRA)
9 rue des Cordelières
75013, Paris
France
http://www.elra.info
Email: lrec@elda.org

Message from the General Chair

This volume documents the Proceedings of the SmiLa2022 Workshop on Smiling and Laughter across Contexts and the Life-span, held on the 24th of June 2022 as part of the LREC 2022 conference (International Conference on Language Resources and Evaluation).

Smiling and Laughter are crucial communicative means in our interaction and can affect importantly the meaning of our utterances, the unfolding of the dialogue, and the relationship between interactants. Previous research provided us with important insights into the role of smiling and laughter in interaction, how they "work" and how to process them. Nevertheless, there are still many open questions and under-explored areas of investigation, which given the multidimensional nature of smiling and laughter need a multidisciplinary approach to be addressed. The main aim of our workshop is therefore to highlight these still unresolved questions encouraging sharing in terms of insights, methods, and resources across domains and fields, in order to further boost the interdisciplinary collaborations which are already intrinsically at the core of the community. As a multidisciplinary workshop, we invited contributors of different backgrounds to share their work revolving around smiling and laughter with the main goal to push further the boundaries reached by previous work, to improve the fluidity of resources exchanges and inter-disciplinary collaborations in order to deepen our understanding of these communicative displays and build applications able to recognise, process, and produce them when desirable.

Organizers

Catherine Pelachaud – CNRS, ISIR, Sorbonne University (FRANCE)
Chiara Mazzocconi – ILCB - LPL, CNRS - Aix-Marseille University (FRANCE)
Gary McKeown – School of Behavioural Sciences, Queen's University Belfast (UK)
Kevin El Haddad – ISIA, University of Mons (BELGIUM)

Program Committee:

Abdellah Fourtassi, INRIA - Paris, Aix-Marseille University (FRANCE)
Andy Lücking, LLF - CNRS, Université de Paris (FRANCE); Text Technology Lab, Goethe University Frankfurt (GERMANY)
Béatrice Priego-Valverde, LPL - CNRS, Aix-Marseille University (FRANCE)
Christine Howes, CLASP, University of Gothenburg (SWEDEN)
Emer Gilmartin, ADAPT Center TCD (IRELAND)
Fabien Ringeval, Grenoble Alps University (FRANCE)
Greg Bryant, Department of Communication, University of California, Los Angeles (U.S.A)
Ilaria Torre, KTH Royal Institute of Technology (SWEDEN)
Isabella Poggi, Department of Philosophy, Communication, and Performing Arts, Roma Tre University, Rome (ITALY)
Jonathan Ginzburg, LLF - CNRS, Université de Paris (FRANCE)
Joni Zhong, Department of Rehabilitation Sciences, The Hong Kong Polytechnic University
Kristiina Jokinen, AI Research Center AIST Tokyo Waterfront (JAPAN)
Magdalena Rychlowska, School of Psychology, Queen's University Belfast (UK)
Pablo Arias Sarah, Lund University, IRCAM, CNRS, Sorbonne Universités (FRANCE)
Paul L. Rosin, Cardiff University (UK)

Table of Contents

Workshop Program

Friday, June 24, 2022

09:00–09:19 Welcoming and SmiLa introduction by Kevin El Haddad and Chiara Mazzocconi

09:19–09:39 Key Note 1 - Gary McKeown

09:39–10:30 Oral Session 1

09:39–09:56 *Toward a Semi-Automated Scoping Review of Virtual Human Smiles*
Sharon Mozgai, Jade Winn, Cari Kaurloto, Andrew Leeds, Dirk Heylen and Arno Hartholt

09:56–10:13 *Are you Smiling When I am Speaking?*
Auriane Boudin, Roxane Bertrand, Magalie Ochs, Philippe Blache and Stephane Rauzy

10:13–10:30 *Gender Differences, Smiling, and Economic Negotiation Outcomes*
Paulina Hiersch, Gary McKeown, Ioana Latu and Magdalena Rychlowska

10:30–11:00 Coffee break

11:00–11:34 Oral Session 2

11:00–11:17 *A Measure of the Smiling Synchrony in the Conversational Face-to-face Interaction Corpus PACO-CHEESE*
Stéphane Rauzy, Mary Amoyal and Béatrice Priego-Valverde

11:17–11:34 *Analysis of Co-Laughter Gesture Relationship on RGB videos in Dyadic Conversation Context*
Hugo Bohy, Ahmad Hammoudeh, Antoine Maiorca, Stéphane Dupont and Thierry Dutoit

11:35–11:55 Key Note 2 - Catherine Pelachaud

11:55–12:50 Poster session + Discussions and networking

11:55–12:50 *You make me laugh! Friends, strangers and neurodiversity*
Ceci Cai, Lucie Vigreux, Manying Chiu, Bangjie Wang, Alexis Macintyre, Sarah White and Sophie Scott

11:55–12:50 *Intergroup Bias in Smile Discrimination in Autism*
Ruihan Wu, Antonia Hamilton and Sarah White

Continued

11:55–12:50 *Inhalation Noises as Endings of Laughs in Conversational Speech*
Jürgen Trouvain, Raphael Werner andKhiet Truong

11:55–12:50 *Are there any body-movement differences between women and men when they laugh?*
Ahmad Hammoudeh, Antoine Maiorca, Stéphane Dupont and Thierry Dutoit

11:55–12:50 *Laughter During Cooperative and Competitive Games*
Magdalena Rychlowska, Gary McKeown, Ian Sneddon and William Curran

12:50–13:00 Closing remarks and way forward

Proceedings of the Smiling and Laughter across Contexts and the Life-span Workshop @LREC2022, pages 1–5
Marseille, 24 June 2022

Toward a Semi-Automated Scoping Review of Virtual Human Smiles

Sharon Mozgai[1], Jade Winn[2], Cari Kaurloto[2], Andrew Leeds[1], Dirk Heylen[3], Arno Hartholt[1]
[1]USC Institute for Creative Technologies, [2]USC Libraries, [3]University of Twente
[1]Playa Vista, CA, USA [2]Los Angeles, CA, USA [3] Enschede, the Netherlands
[1]{mozgai, leeds, hartholt}@ict.usc.edu
[2]{jadewinn, cari.kaurloto}@usc.edu
[3]d.k.j.heylen@utwente.nl

Abstract

Smiles are a fundamental facial expression for successful human-agent communication. The growing number of publications in this domain presents an opportunity for future research and design to be informed by a scoping review of the extant literature. This semi-automated review expedites the first steps toward the mapping of Virtual Human (VH) smile research. This paper contributes an overview of the status quo of VH smile research, identifies research streams through cluster analysis, identifies prolific authors in the field, and provides evidence that a full scoping review is needed to synthesize the findings in the expanding domain of VH smile research. To enable collaboration, we provide full access to the refined *VH smile dataset*, key word and author word clouds, as well as interactive evidence maps.

Keywords: human language technologies, machine learning, embodied conversational agents, virtual humans, datasets

1. Introduction

Virtual humans (VHs) are digitally embodied characters designed to simulate face-to-face human interaction. In contrast to chatbots that primarily rely on text or language-based technologies, VHs can employ additional communicative modalities, including the paralinguistic aspects of the voice (e.g., prosody or voice quality), as well as gesture and facial expressions (Wu et al., 2018; Hartholt et al., 2019b; Gordon et al., 2019; Mell et al., 2020). A fundamental facial expression for successful human-agent communication, capable of impacting the interpretation of dialogue and modulating the relationship between interlocutors, is smiling (Heylen, 2003; Ochs et al., 2013; Chu et al., 2019).

Numerous publications explore the complex topic of VH smiles and span a broad range of research areas; for example, the modeling and generation of VH smiles, rapport building, mimicry, perception, and social signal processing (Obaid et al., 2010; Pelachaud, 2017; Gratch et al., 2006; Prepin et al., 2012; Ochs et al., 2017). This diverse literature, unsurprisingly, includes a wide variety of applications, study designs, and outcome variables. Previous scoping reviews have been inclusive of VH smiles as part of a larger research aim, such as surveying the use of VH facial expressions in prosocial design (Oliveira et al., 2021). However, no prior reviewers have specifically isolated and examined the breadth of extant VH smile literature.

A need remains to systematically bring together this multi-disciplinary research to (1) map the vast body of literature on VH smiles, (2) identify gaps to inform future research, and (3) guide VH design. Toward these aims, while managing the diffuse nature of this literature, we adopted a semi-automated scoping review methodology to rapidly mine an existing primary VH document dataset. This *VH dataset* was compiled by our research team and spans the previous 30 years of VH research. Here we present our first steps toward a semi-automated scoping review of the VH smile literature and make the following contributions:

- Introduce our primary *VH dataset* of 32,924 pieces of published primary research as well as the distillation of the *VH smile dataset* of 76 articles.
- Present our document mining approach to increase the speed of article identification and mapping of the domain.
- Discover and describe topic clusters within the *VH smile dataset.*
- Identify prolific researchers in the field of VH smile research.

The remainder of this paper is organized as follows. The next section describes the scoping review datasets included in the analysis, details the leveraged methodology to collect and collate the documents, and outlines the semi-automated approach employed to facilitate this review. The third section provides specific results for the *VH smile dataset*. The final section discusses the results of our work, defines the limitations of our research and outlines next steps. To enable collaboration, we provide full access to the *VH smile dataset* inclusive of paper titles, abstracts, authors, and document embeddings, as well as generated word clouds and interactive evidence maps.[1]

2. Methods

The here presented work is part of the Virtual Human Fidelity Coalition (VHFC), a collaboration between the

[1]`https://github.com/USC-ICT/VHFC`

Name	Search Terms	Range	Found	Included
VH dataset	virtual human(s), embodied conversation agent(s), virtual agent(s), digital human(s)	1990-2021	60,640	32,934
VH smile dataset	(virtual human(s), embodied conversation agent(s), virtual agent(s), digital human(s)) AND smile)	1999-2021	498	76

Table 1: *VH* and *VH smile datasets*. Resources collected from these databases: ACM, ArXiv, Ebsco, Engineering Village, IEEE Xplore, Gale Computer, Proquest, PubMed, ScienceDirect, Scopus, Wiley, and Web of Science.

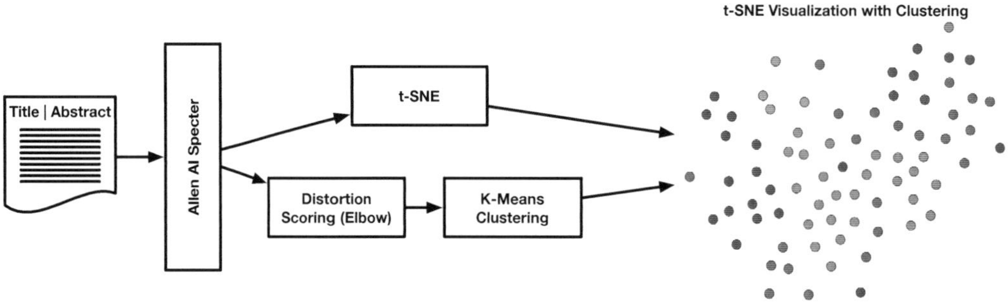

Figure 1: Approach overview. A collection of all papers' titles and abstracts are processed through SPECTER to derive high-dimensional semantic embeddings of each paper. To visualize the data in two-dimensional representation we leverage t-SNE, while the high-dimensional embeddings are evaluated and clustered on a separate path. Lastly, the cluster assignments are used to color each data point in the two-dimensional representation.

University of Southern California Institute for Creative Technologies and USC Libraries. The overarching goal of the VHFC is to explore and catalog research on virtual human fidelity across multidisciplinary domains to drive the efficiency of future VH design while maximizing the efficacy of VH intervention outcomes.

As a first step in the project, two expert information specialists conducted comprehensive literature searches in consultation with our research team. We searched 12 electronic databases from 1990 to 2021 to create a primary *VH dataset* of the previous 30 years of VH research. Initial inclusion criteria for this review considered: journal articles, conference proceedings, and grey literature such as dissertations and theses, and review articles published in English. Articles that centered on robots or conversational agents without embodiment were excluded. The search strategy was not limited by study design. Multiple search terms for VHs were employed: VH, virtual agent, and embodied conversational agents are popular terms in the academic literature, while digital human is often used in industry. A summary of databases, search terms, date ranges, total number of works found (i.e., before removing duplicates or incomplete entries) and total number of included publications is provided in Table 1.

A total of 60,640 resources were retrieved and uploaded into the online systematic review software, Covidence. The software's automatic de-duplicating feature removed 26,487 resources. Additionally, we cleaned the data of any missing data points, leaving 32,934 papers in the *VH dataset*. A subset of this *VH dataset* was created using all possible tenses of the search terms *smile* to mine document titles and abstracts. Following the same de-duping process, a dataset of 141 VH smile articles was collected. Level 1 screening (i.e., titles and abstracts) of the *VH smile dataset* was conducted by two trained reviewers. Articles were excluded that did not include (1) VHs, ECAs, virtual agents, or digital humans and (2) smiles or smiling, resulting in a final *VH smile dataset* of 76 documents. We present our semi-automated document-mining approach of these 76 articles to rapidly map the field of VH smiles and provide evidence that this domain warrants a full scoping review.

2.1. Semi-Automated Data Mining Approach

To visualize the complex relationships between papers and to discover prolific authors and topic clusters within this unstructured document dataset, we employed a multi-step process visualized in Figure 1. We leveraged the state-of-the-art document-level representation learning method SPECTER pre-trained directly on paper titles and abstracts as well as their citation-relationships to derive dense high-dimensional numeric representations for each document (Cohan et al., 2020). Next, we employed t-SNE, a dimensionality reduction algorithm to render the high-dimensional embeddings on a two-dimensional interactive mapping, enabling the visual inspection of the relationships between papers (Van der Maaten and Hinton, 2008). As it is difficult for

ID	Cluster Label	Keywords	# Pubs
0	Socio-Emotional State Displays	stance, straight face, facial changes, social context, state display, alignment	12
1	Signal Processing	emotion recognition, social signals, audiovisual fusion, feature, turn	4
2	Social Effects	social, emotion, study, user impressions, trust, mimicry, interaction feedback	13
3	Modeling Social Behavior	behavior, human-agent social interactions, emotion, personality, behavior	13
4	Deployed VHs	museum guide, recommender, pedagogical agent, application, friendliness	7
5	3D Facial Modeling	vectors, 3D, facial expression synthesis, mapping, model, parameter	7
6	Rubbish Bin	N/A	4
7	Virtual Patient	virtual patient, clinical, photorealistic, incisor	1
8	Animation	animation, genuine smile generation, facial, motion, temporal, dynamic	9
9	Deception	lying, truth, deceit, cooperation, trustworthy, lie, deceivers, truth tellers	6

Table 2: *VH smile dataset* clusters derived by word cloud analysis and manual coding of paper titles and abstracts.

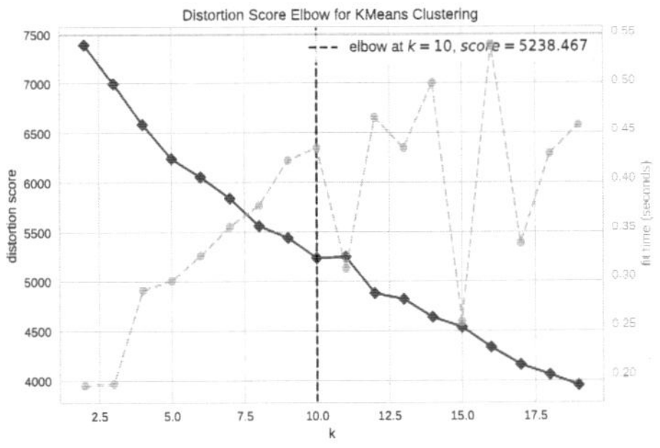

Figure 2: Visualization of k-Elbow distortion metric for optimal k in k-Means clustering.

the human mind to derive meaning and relationships of a high-dimensional representation of the document-embeddings, t-SNE enables two-dimensional visualization of the data while maintaining complex non-linear relationships between the datapoints.[2] To identify the number of research topics and their cluster entries within the vast field of VH smile research we employed the elbow method (Fig. 2) to optimally identify k for the k-means clustering (Kodinariya and Makwana, 2013; Ahmed et al., 2020). In our analysis, we ran the clustering for k ∈ [2,20] in the *VH smile dataset*. For each value of k we calculate the sum of squared errors (SSE) as the distortion score and selected the elbow, or optimal number of clusters, as the trade-off value between an optimal SSE and a small k.

Following this we identified the topic of each cluster leveraging word cloud analysis (Cui et al., 2010). Before running the algorithm[3] we removed common words known as stopwords (e.g., a, do, get, she, I, etc.) to render the word cloud plots more meaningful and focused on the actual topic rather than just common English words.[4] Additionally, we removed words that were likely to be common to all clusters due to our search strategy (i.e., search terms in Table 1). Once the word clouds (Fig. 3) were rendered, two coders independently (1) reviewed each plot to identify keywords and (2) conducted a manual review of the titles and abstracts in each cluster. Meaningful cluster labels were derived through team discussion and reconciliation of the independently derived codes (see Table 2). While the process of naming the clusters may be somewhat subjective, the access to a reproducible, digestible, and quantitative algorithm such as the word cloud algorithm renders this process transparent and efficient, while double coding and team discussion aims to decrease individual bias. Finally, we utilized word cloud analysis to visualize prolific authors in the *VH smile dataset* and in each of the topic clusters.

3. Results

To map the domain of VH smile research, we determined the optimal number of clusters to be k = 10 for the *VH smile dataset*. Manual review of word clouds for each cluster (Fig. 3) as well as the coding of the associated paper titles and abstracts were synthesized to derive representative cluster names and related key terms (Table 2). The highest populated clusters include papers in the following research streams: Cluster 3 *Modeling Social Behavior* (n=13), Cluster 2 *Social Effects* of VH smiles in agent-human interaction (n=13), and Cluster 1 *Socio-Emotional State Displays* (n=12). Of the ten derived clusters, Cluster 6, affectionately labeled our "rubbish bin" captured errors in the manual coding of the possible 141 articles in the *VH smile dataset* aggregating duplicate and irrelevant articles (e.g., robotics). Additionally, Cluster 7 *Virtual Patient* only contains one paper. Manual review of this cluster determined this paper could be incorporated into Cluster 4 *Deployed VHs*, resulting in eight

[2]We utilize the SciKitLearn implementation of t-SNE with the default parameter setting and a random seed of 0 for reproducibility: `https://scikit-learn.org/stable/modules/generated/sklearn.manifold.TSNE.html`

[3]We use a common Python word cloud package: `https://github.com/amueller/word_cloud`

[4]We use the standard stopword dictionary that accompanies the Python implementation of the word cloud library.

Figure 3: Visualization of keywords found in Cluster 1 *Signal Processing* abstracts.

Figure 4: Visualization of prolific authors found in the full *VH smiles dataset*.

Figure 5: Visualization of prolific authors in Cluster 5 *3D Facial Modeling*.

distinct research streams. After defining the clusters, we moved on to word cloud visualization of prolific authors in the overarching *VH smile dataset* (Fig. 4) and topic-specific clusters (Fig. 5) to further map the field and identify the major contributors in each area.

4. Discussion

This semi-automated review leveraged the resources in the preexisting *VH dataset* to expedite the first steps toward the mapping of VH smile literature. This initial investigation (1) identifies and catalogues research streams concentrated in multidisciplinary topic clusters, (2) brings to the forefront key themes and prolific authors within each topic cluster, and (3) provides evidence that a full scoping review is warranted to further map the field, aggregate research findings, and identify

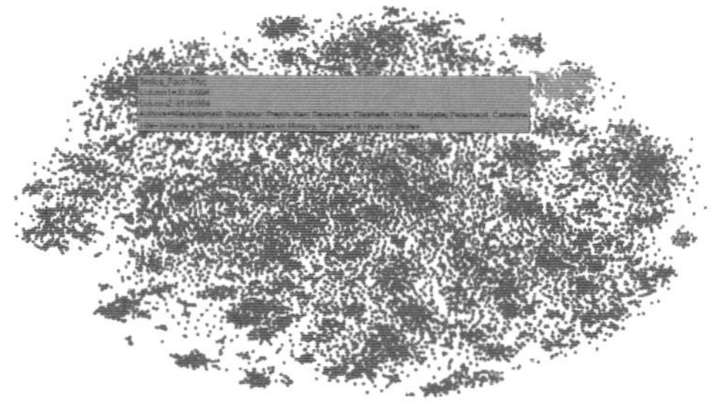

Figure 6: Interactive map of all documents (orange) when the search terms *smile(s)(ed)(ing)* and *facial expression(s)* are applied to the *VH dataset* (blue).

gaps in the current research.

A limitation of our rapid semi-automated review was the use of the specific search term *smile* within the *VH dataset* ultimately yielding only 76 relevant articles for analysis. For the second phase of this work, a planned scoping review, we will expand our investigation to include the search term *facial expression(s)*. An initial review of the *VH dataset* with these added terms revealed 1,206 articles to be included in level 1 screening (Fig. 6). Additionally, while the methodology presented above provided a quick and useful snapshot of the field and a database of relevant papers organized by topic cluster, a full scoping review following the guidelines outlined by Arksey and O'Malley, would take the important next steps in systematically synthesizing empirical results and reporting on aggregate findings (Arksey and O'Malley, 2005).

The adoption and deployment of VHs across multiple contexts such as education, healthcare, military, real estate, customer service, marketing, and sales to automate and innovate tasks is at an all-time high and continues to rise due to the contributions of major game engines, accessibility to the 5G network, and the rise of the metaverse (Ludusan and Wagner, 2021; Hartholt et al., 2019a; Ma et al., 2019; Burden and Savin-Baden, 2019; Martha and Santoso, 2019; Endicott, 2021). Studies of human interaction often consider smile dynamics, however, this feature is frequently lacking in complexity and intentional design in VHs, presenting an opportunity to provide evidence-based recommendations for future research and design informed by a full scoping review of the extant VH smile literature.

5. Acknowledgements

Part of the efforts depicted were sponsored by the US Army under contract W911NF-14-D-0005. The content of the information does not necessarily reflect the position or the policy of the Government, and no official endorsement should be inferred.

6. Bibliographical References

Ahmed, M., Seraj, R., and Islam, S. M. S. (2020). The k-means algorithm: A comprehensive survey and performance evaluation. *Electronics*, 9(8):1295.

Arksey, H. and O'Malley, L. (2005). Scoping studies: towards a methodological framework. *International journal of social research methodology*, 8(1):19–32.

Burden, D. and Savin-Baden, M. (2019). *Virtual humans: Today and tomorrow*. Chapman and Hall/CRC.

Chu, V. C., Lucas, G. M., Lei, S., Mozgai, S., Khooshabeh, P., and Gratch, J. (2019). Emotion regulation in the prisoner's dilemma: effects of reappraisal on behavioral measures and cardiovascular measures of challenge and threat. *Frontiers in human neuroscience*, 13:50.

Cohan, A., Feldman, S., Beltagy, I., Downey, D., and Weld, D. S. (2020). Specter: Document-level representation learning using citation-informed transformers. *arXiv preprint arXiv:2004.07180*.

Cui, W., Wu, Y., Liu, S., Wei, F., Zhou, M. X., and Qu, H. (2010). Context preserving dynamic word cloud visualization. In *2010 IEEE Pacific Visualization Symposium (PacificVis)*, pages 121–128. IEEE.

Endicott, M. L. (2021). Virtual human systems: A generalised model.

Gordon, C., Leuski, A., Benn, G., Klassen, E., Fast, E., Liewer, M., Hartholt, A., and Traum, D. R. (2019). Primer: An emotionally aware virtual agent.

Gratch, J., Okhmatovskaia, A., Lamothe, F., Marsella, S., Morales, M., van der Werf, R. J., and Morency, L.-P. (2006). Virtual rapport. In *International Workshop on Intelligent Virtual Agents*, pages 14–27. Springer.

Hartholt, A., Fast, E., Reilly, A., Whitcup, W., Liewer, M., and Mozgai, S. (2019a). Ubiquitous virtual humans: A multi-platform framework for embodied ai agents in xr. In *2019 IEEE International Conference on Artificial Intelligence and Virtual Reality (AIVR)*, pages 308–3084. IEEE.

Hartholt, A., Mozgai, S., and Rizzo, A. S. (2019b). Virtual job interviewing practice for high-anxiety populations. In *Proceedings of the 19th ACM International Conference on Intelligent Virtual Agents*, pages 238–240.

Heylen, D. (2003). Facial expressions for conversational agents. In *N. Suzuki and C. Bartneck Subtle Expressivity for Characters and Robots. CHI 2003 Workshop (www. bartneck. de/workshop/chi3003)*.

Kodinariya, T. M. and Makwana, P. R. (2013). Review on determining number of cluster in k-means clustering. *International Journal*, 1(6):90–95.

Ludusan, B. and Wagner, P. (2021). Knock-knock! who's there? the laughter-enhanced virtual real-estate agent. In *Elektronische Sprachsignalverarbeitung 2021. Tagungsband der 32. Konferenz*.

Ma, T., Sharifi, H., and Chattopadhyay, D. (2019). Virtual humans in health-related interventions: A meta-analysis. In *Extended Abstracts of the 2019 CHI Conference on Human Factors in Computing Systems*, pages 1–6.

Martha, A. S. D. and Santoso, H. B. (2019). The design and impact of the pedagogical agent: A systematic literature review. *Journal of Educators Online*, 16(1):n1.

Mell, J., Lucas, G., Mozgai, S., and Gratch, J. (2020). The effects of experience on deception in human-agent negotiation. *Journal of Artificial Intelligence Research*, 68:633–660.

Obaid, M., Mukundan, R., Billinghurst, M., and Pelachaud, C. (2010). Expressive mpeg-4 facial animation using quadratic deformation models. In *2010 Seventh International Conference on Computer Graphics, Imaging and Visualization*, pages 9–14. IEEE.

Ochs, M., Pelachaud, C., and Prepin, K. (2013). Social stances by virtual smiles. In *2013 14th International Workshop on Image Analysis for Multimedia Interactive Services (WIAMIS)*, pages 1–4. IEEE.

Ochs, M., Pelachaud, C., and Mckeown, G. (2017). A user perception–based approach to create smiling embodied conversational agents. *ACM Transactions on Interactive Intelligent Systems (TiiS)*, 7(1):1–33.

Oliveira, R., Arriaga, P., Santos, F. P., Mascarenhas, S., and Paiva, A. (2021). Towards prosocial design: A scoping review of the use of robots and virtual agents to trigger prosocial behaviour. *Computers in Human Behavior*, 114:106547.

Pelachaud, C. (2017). Conversing with social agents that smile and laugh. In *INTERSPEECH*, page 2052.

Prepin, K., Ochs, M., and Pelachaud, C. (2012). Mutual stance building in dyad of virtual agents: Smile alignment and synchronisation. In *2012 International Conference on Privacy, Security, Risk and Trust and 2012 International Confernece on Social Computing*, pages 938–943. IEEE.

Van der Maaten, L. and Hinton, G. (2008). Visualizing data using t-sne. *Journal of machine learning research*, 9(11).

Wu, J., Ghosh, S., Chollet, M., Ly, S., Mozgai, S., and Scherer, S. (2018). Nadia: Neural network driven virtual human conversation agents. In *Proceedings of the 18th International Conference on Intelligent Virtual Agents*, pages 173–178.

Proceedings of the Smiling and Laughter across Contexts and the Life-span Workshop @LREC2022, pages 6–10
Marseille, 24 June 2022

Are you Smiling When I am Speaking?

Auriane Boudin[1,2], Roxane Bertrand[1], Magalie Ochs[2], Philippe Blache[1], Stéphane Rauzy[1]
[1] LPL, CNRS & Aix-Marseille University
[2] LIS, CNRS & Aix-Marseille University
{auriane.boudin, roxane.bertrand, magalie.ochs, philippe.blache, stephane.rauzy, }@univ-amu.fr

Abstract

The aim of this study is to investigate conversational feedback that contains smiles and laughter. Firstly, we propose a statistical analysis of smiles and laughter used as generic and specific feedback in a corpus of French talk-in-interaction. Our results show that smiles of low intensity are preferentially used to produce generic feedback while high intensity smiles and laughter are preferentially used to produce specific feedback. Secondly, based on a machine learning approach, we propose a two-stage classification of feedback to automatically predict not only the presence/absence of a smile but, also the type of smile according to an intensity-scale (low or high).

Keywords: Conversational feedback, Smile, Laughter, Corpus study, Generic/Specific feedback

1. Introduction

During conversations, interlocutors switch dynamically between the role of speaker and listener. The speaker produces discourse, giving information to the listener who produces *feedback* (referred as FB)[1] to show his/her active listening (Schegloff, 1982) but also to contribute to the elaboration of the current discourse (Bavelas et al., 2000; Horton, 2017). FB promotes alignment between interlocutors, which allows the success of the interaction (Pickering and Garrod, 2013). FB production is also studied in part to render human-machine conversations more efficient (Glas and Pelachaud, 2015).

Following (Bavelas et al., 2000), **generic FB** (e.g. *"mhmh", "okay"*, nod) is used to show understanding, while **specific FB** (e.g. *"oh really", "that's so nice"*) is used to show assessment through diverse attitudes (Schegloff, 1982; Bavelas et al., 2000; Horton, 2017). Both generic and specific FB can be unimodal or bimodal (vocal *and/or* visual). In this work, we focus on FB that contains smiles and laughter (associated with verbalization and/or nods).

In this study, we first propose to explore how smiles and laughter are distributed according to the generic and specific FB dichotomy. Next, we present a two-stage classification to automatically predict smile in FB instances. The 1st stage of classification will predict whether a FB should be realized with a smile or a neutral face. The 2nd stage of classification will predict for FB with a smile, the intensity of the smile (high or low). We make use of the open-access corpus PACO (Amoyal et al., 2020) and Cheese! (Priego-Valverde et al., 2020) to investigate multimodal FB. Through a statistical analysis and a machine learning approach on a conversational corpus, we explore the 2 following hypotheses. (1) High intensity smiles are more salient in the discourse and should be preferentially used to show assessments or specific attitudes rather than understanding. Indeed, specific FB is generally more marked than generic FB. Consequently, **Neutral Faces (NF)** and **Low Intensity Smiles (LI Smiles)** should be preferentially used to produce generic FB while **High Intensity Smiles (HI Smiles)** and laughter should be preferentially used to produce specific FB. (2) Listeners are influenced by the main speaker behavior and tend to align during FB production by adopting similar conversational markers (e.g. same smile intensity). Given the mechanism of alignment, the prediction of the smile and the intensity of the smile during a FB realization should be derived from the smile annotation of the speaker (Heerey and Crossley, 2013). In consequence, we expect to observe an important quantity of FB produced by the listener with a smile intensity similar to the one expressed by the main speaker.

2. Related Works

Feedback shows the collaboration between a speaker and an interlocutor during interactions (Schegloff, 1982). According to (Bavelas et al., 2000), interlocutors can produce two types of FB: **generic** and **specific**. Generic FB shows understanding and is mostly realized with a nod and/or short vocalizations (e.g. *"yeah", "mhmh"*). On their side, specific FB is closely connected to the semantic content. It occurs once the common ground is established, when the listener has enough information to react with particular elements (wince, exclamation, rising tone) that can show *surprise, amusement, enthusiasm, etc.* (Tolins and Tree, 2014). Specific FB can be realized with variable elements such as *lexicalization, laughter, head movements, eyebrow movements, facial expressions, etc.*.

Following the generic/specific dichotomy, we propose a fine-grained classification for specific FB by adding two sub-levels (Boudin et al., 2021). The 1st level corresponds to the *polarity*: *positive* or *negative*. This polarity refers to the semantic content produced by the main speaker (e.g. a positive FB can respond to a fun story and a negative FB to a critic). The

[1](also called *conversational feedback* or *backchannel*)

2nd level concerns the *expected* or *unexpected* aspect of the information given to the listener. The expected/unexpected category refers to the transmission of information. The main speaker can refer to the common ground, i.e. the information already shared with the listener (expected) or she/he can also give new information to the listener (unexpected). These two levels of specific FB allow to classify different attitudes expressed by FB (enthusiasm, happiness, humor, compassion, embarrassment, critic). Within each sub-category (positive-expected, positive-unexpected, negative-expected, negative-unexpected), we infer that FB could be realized with some typical patterns (e.g. a rising intonation, with a smile and raised eyebrows for a positive-unexpected FB). In this work we focus on the different types of smiles used within each type and sub-type of FB.

To our knowledge, there is few systematic studies on smiling and its role as FB. Smiles have been identified as a part of FB form quite early (Brunner, 1979). (Duncan et al., 1979) observe that the listener's FB has a greater probability to be produced with a smile if the speaker is actually smiling. (Allwood and Cerrato, 2003) investigate FB functions and point out that smiles are frequently used to produce acknowledgments and clarification requests. Smiles can also show a reinforcement of a positive attitude. Among few studies, (Jensen, 2015) look at smiles and laughter as FB. In their data 33.3% of smiles and 18.6% of laughter is used as FB.

Note that as far as we know, there are few research works which attempt to predict automatically smiles in FB production. (Kok and Heylen, 2011) predict 3 types of smiles (*amused, polite* and *embarrassed*) during conversation with a Conditional Random Fields (CRF) algorithm. Four models are trained and evaluated to predict smiles and the type of smile. However, the prediction scores remain low, with f-score under 0.20.

(El Haddad et al., 2016) predict smiles and laughter FB with different intensity levels. A CRF model is trained accepting as input features laughter and smiles of different intensities produced both by the speaker and the listener. The predicted FB instances are implemented in a virtual agent and compared with different baselines. A subjective evaluation leads to satisfying and promising results.

3. Corpus & Method

PACO-Cheese! Corpus We used the French Cheese! and PACO corpora. They contain a total of 7 hours of audio-visual recording of 26 dyadic face-to-face interactions, lasting between 15 and 20 minutes. In the current work a subset of 13 dyads (3.6 hours) is used, on which instances of FB have been annotated.

The full set of available annotations is described in (Priego-Valverde et al., 2020; Amoyal et al., 2020; Boudin et al., 2021). Laughter has been manually annotated during the transcription process. In (Amoyal and Priego-Valverde, 2019; Rauzy and Amoyal, 2020; Amoyal et al., 2020), smiles have been annotated with 5 labels from the smile intensity scale (SIS) proposed by (Gironzetti et al., 2016): *S0* (neutral face), *S1* (close mouth smile), *S2* (open mouth smile), *S3* (wide open mouth smile), *S4* (laughing smile). S4 are mainly associated with vocal laughter. Regions between two vocal laughter could also be annotated S4 if the facial posture did not change. On their side, laughter is vocal elements that can be produced with neutral face or smile of lower intensity. Therefore, there is not a one-to-one correspondence between the two entities and we prefer to distinguish both laughter and S4 in the current work. Instances of FB have been annotated following the 5 labels described in section 2: *generic, positive-expected, positive-unexpected, negative-expected* and *negative-unexpected*. They are reactions from one speaker to the other speaker's speech and can be composed of verbalization, nods, laughter and smile or a combination of these elements.

Logistic regression We used a Logistic Regression algorithm (Logit). The Logit models the probability that a FB occurs with a smile (and its associated intensity level). It allows to evaluate the specific contribution of each feature which facilitates the interpretation of the model. The Logit proves also to be relevant when dealing with small datasets. A binary classifier response is obtained from the Logit probability, by applying a probability threshold filter.

While in (Boudin et al., 2021) we aimed at predicting the position and the type of FB, in the current research work we consider that the position and the type of the FB is already known and we focus on the prediction of one element of the FB form: smile.

For that, we propose a two-stage classification where the 1st stage predicts the presence or absence of a smile in the FB form (993 FB with a neutral face and 1372 FB with a smile). The 2nd stage predicts the intensity of the smile (high or low) for the subset of FB containing a smile. In order to obtain balanced classes, the S1 and S2 smiles have been grouped as **LI Smiles** (361 FB with 'S1' and 284 FB with 'S2') and S3 and S4 as **HI Smiles** (188 FB with 'S3' and 539 FB with 'S4'). The dataset is composed of all the annotated FB with the associated smile used to produce it. When different smiles are used to produce the FB, we keep only the smile with the highest intensity. A prediction is correct if the item that composed the FB predicted matches with the item that composed the observed FB. A cross-validation has been obtained by running a Monte Carlo cross-validation (on 50 trials with a ratio 80%-20% for the training versus the evaluation sample) for both models. For comparison, two baseline models are computed that randomly predict the class according to the observed corpus frequency for the 2 distributions: smile/no-smile and LI/HI Smiles. Features are extracted from the speaker signal before the listener's FB. The subset of multi-modal features (a total of 16 features) is based on our previous analysis in (Boudin et al., 2021) to predict the FB type:

- Pause (presence or absence of silent pauses, before FB). Overlap (FB is produced during the speech of the main speaker) - Binary encoding (0: absence, 1: presence).
- Positive, Negative, Concrete tokens (that give potential cues about the FB sub-type) (Bonin et al., 2018) - Categorical encoding: counted since the last FB produced.
- Interjection, Discourse markers, Punctuation (Rauzy et al., 2014). Extracted in a previous window of 2 seconds and binary encoding. Number of tokens in the previous 2 seconds - Categorical encoding.
- Nod, Smiles (S1, S2, S3, S4, S0), Laughter - Extracted in a previous window of 2 seconds ; binary encoding.

4. Results & Discussion

4.1. Laughter and Smiles for FB Production

A total of 2,380 instances of FB was annotated: 1,207 generic and 1,173 specific, including 416 positive-expected, 550 positive-unexpected, 115 negative-expected, 92 negative-unexpected. During the 13 interactions, we report a total of 1215 'S0' , 1014 'S1', 944 'S2', 729 'S3', 798 'S4', among smiles 40% are used inside FB. 1051 laughter has been annotated (including 417 as FB).

20% of FB is produced with more than one intensity of smiles (e.g. *"yeah exactly"* that begins with a S0, continues with S1 and ends in S4). Among these instances of FB with particular smile's pattern, the majority (66%) shows an increasing smile intensity.

Figure 1 presents the smile intensities and laughter used to produce FB according to their generic/specific type[2] Figure 2 details the smiles and laughter for sub-types of specific FB.

All FB: Globally, 42.35% of FB is produced with a Neutral face (NF). S1, S2, S3 and S4 are equally used (27% for S1/S2, 30% for S3/S4). 17.52% of FB is produced with a laughter. Only 9.87% of FB is realized with a smile or a laughter alone. The rest of the time, FB is associated with verbalization, nods or others facial movements. Note that at least 71% of FB annotations in our corpus are multimodal[3].

Generic FB : NF (58.58%) is mostly used to produce generic FB. Regarding FB produced with a smile, the more the intensity of the smile increases, the more its use decreases. Generic FB rarely contains a laughter (1.74%).

[2]When several smiles are used, only the one with the highest intensity is counted.

[3]Our annotations did not contain eyebrow movements, nor other head movements than nods, nor facial expressions. With these annotations, the percentage of multimodal FB would be probably be higher

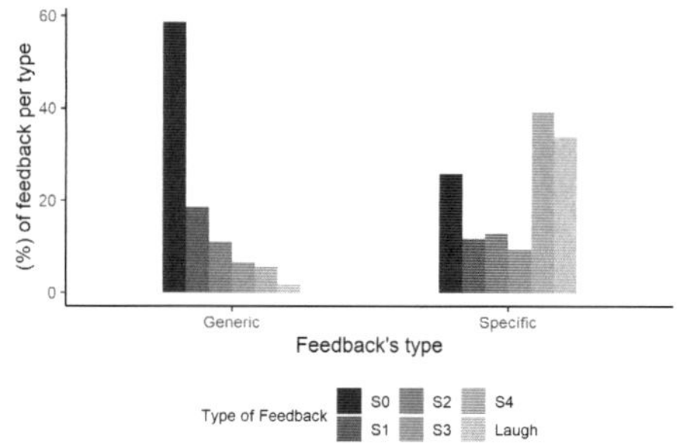

Figure 1: *Generic and Specific FB produced with Neutral face (S0), Smiles according to their intensity level (S1, S2, S3, S4) and laughter. When a FB contains plural smiles, only the highest intensity is kept.*

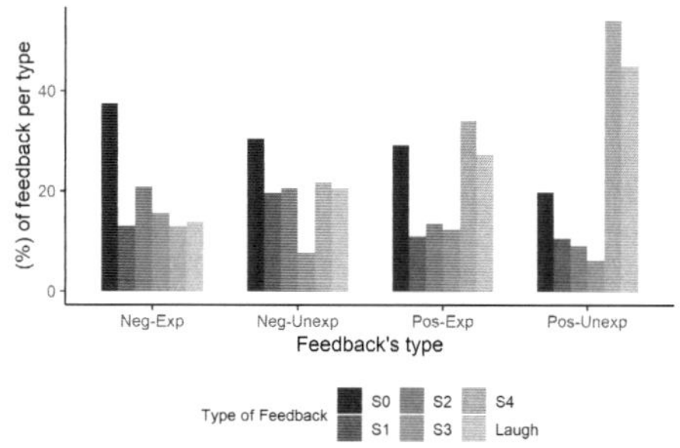

Figure 2: *Specific FB (Positive-Expected, Positive-Unexpected, Negative-Expected, Negative-Unexpected) produced with Neutral face (S0), Smiles according to their intensity level (S1, S2, S3, S4) and laughter. When a FB contains plural smiles, only the highest intensity is kept.*

Specific FB: Only 25.66% of specific FB is produced with a NF. 24.55% are produced with a LI Smile. 48.65% of specific FB is produced with a HI Smile. 33.76% contain a laughter. Laughter and HI Smiles are more present for positive FB, specifically for unexpected ones compared to negative FB. Concerning negative FB, NF is preferentially used, especially for the expected ones. Nonetheless, as we expected, smiles are still present for negative FB since smiles can be used to show embarrassment or compassion.

These observations confirm our 1st hypothesis: NF and LI Smiles are mainly used to produce generic FB whereas LI Smiles and laughter are mainly used to produce specific FB. These observations support our typology of FB, particularly useful to characterize the form of FB.

4.2. Speaker & Listener alignment

There are various ways to evaluate alignment between interlocutors (Rauzy et al., 2022). Herein, we focus on the alignment between the listeners and the speakers by looking at the smiles and laughter produced both as FB (by the listener) and as features (by the speaker in a window of 2s before the FB). For each level of smiles defined above, we compute 3 quantities: the proportion P_{FB} of FB containing the given level among all

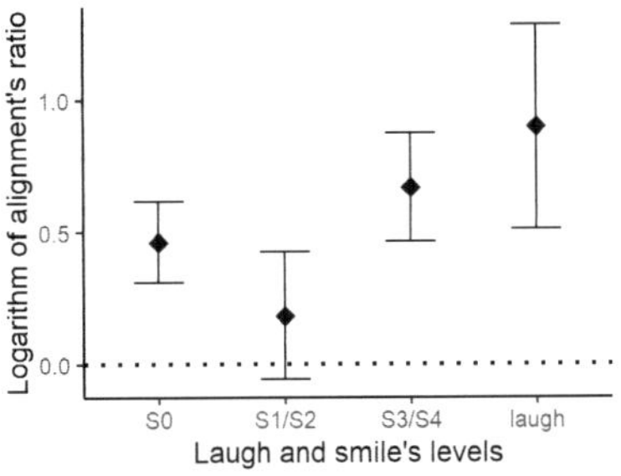

Figure 3: *Logarithm of allgnment's ratio for NF (S0), LI Smile (S1/S2), HI Smile (S3/S4) and Laughter between the speaker and the listener.*

the FB, the proportion P_{Feat} of features containing the given level and the proportion $P_{FB/Feat}$ of pair of features/FB containing conjointly the given level. The first two quantities allow to compute the proportion of co-occurrences by chance. We define the alignment's ratio as the ratio of the observed proportion $P_{FB/Feat}$ to the proportion expected by chance $P_{FB} \times P_{Feat}$. Figure 3 presents the logarithm of the alignment's ratio and its associated 2σ standard error bars for NF, LI Smiles, HI Smiles and Laughter.

We observe a significant alignment for all the group except for the LI Smiles, particularly for laughter and HI Smiles. These results confirm our 2nd hypothesis about alignment, except for LI Smiles. Nonetheless, LI Smiles are visually more subtle, which can explain that they are less employed in the alignment strategy.

4.3. Logit

The 1st model predicts smiles in FB. The 2nd model predicts the smile intensity. The performances and the selected features are presented in Table 1 and 2.

Smile prediction: The 1st model provides accurate performances, significantly better than the baseline (t-test provided a p-value < 0.001). All smiles intensity levels are selected as features by the Logit and multi-modal features appear significant. To estimate the importance of multi-modality, we test the models with only smiles features. For the 1st model, a t-test (p-value < 0.05) confirms that multimodal features perform better than smile features alone.

Smile intensity prediction: The 2nd fine-grained model gives reliable scores, better than the baseline (t-test provided a p-value < 0.001). Only NF and HI Smiles are selected, which are the most extreme smile intensity. This suggests that the most salient markers produced by the main speaker are the most informative for choosing the smile intensity. Removing the other multi-modal features does not significantly alters the performance obtained when using only smile features. These results suggest that not only smiles but also contextual parameters (speaker activity and semantic polarity) are relevant to decide whether a FB should be produced with a smile or not. Once the listener has decided if a smile will compose his/her FB, NF and HI

Pred	F	P	R
Smile	**0.72**	0.83	0.64
Smile Baseline	0.57	0.57	0.57
Intensity	**0.66**	0.72	0.61
Intensity Baseline	0.48	0.48	0.48

Table 1: F-score (F), Precision (P) and Recall (R) for the two predictive models and their baseline.

Pred	Features
Smile	S4, S3, S1, S0, S2, Overlap, Laughter, Pause, Positive Token
Smile intensity	S4, Overlap, Discourse marker, S0, S3

Table 2: Features selected by the *Logit* for the two classification tasks: smile/non smile and LI Smile/HI Smile prediction. Features presented are those selected by the Logit and ranked by their order of importance.

Smile are sufficient enough to choose the smile intensity, through mechanisms of alignment. Finally, these results are in line with our 2nd hypothesis, indicating that the smiles from the speaker are a good predictor of the smiles produced by the listener.

5. Conclusion

In this work, we focused on smiles and laughter as conversational FB in French face-to-face conversation. The data reveal that neutral faces (NF), Low Intensity Smiles (LI Smiles) and High Intensity Smiles (HI Smiles) are used to produce both generic and specific FB. Nonetheless, some trends emerge. Our analysis highlights that generic FB is preferentially produced with NF and LI Smiles, while specific FB, especially positive FB, are preferentially produced with laughter and HI smiles. The same behavior is observed for unexpected FB. For negative FB the trend in the different intensity of smiles stays unclear and need deepest investigations. To better understand it, we could analyse the smiles functions (e.g. embarrassment, compassion, showing sympathy) (Hoque et al., 2011; Mazzocconi et al., 2020). Alignment between the speaker and the listener is measured for NF, HI Smiles and laughter. Laughter is the behavior that is the most reproduced by the listener when it is produced by the speaker. Finally, we presented a hierarchical classifier method to predict smiles and their intensity for FB production, that obtains reliable performances. The model also indicates that the smile intensity features play an important role in the prediction which confirms our results on alignment. The current work come along with a larger project about the prediction of the FB position and the type of FB. Ultimately, it will provide a complete model including the prediction of localization, types and multimodal component of FB allowing the implementation in an effective dialog system, see for example (El Haddad et al., 2016).

6. Acknowlodgments

Research supported by grants ANR-16-CONV-0002 (ILCB) and the Excellence Initiative of Aix-Marseille University (A*MIDEX).

7. Bibliographical References

Allwood, J. and Cerrato, L. (2003). A study of gestural feedback expressions. In *First nordic symposium on multimodal communication*, pages 7–22. Copenhagen.

Amoyal, M. and Priego-Valverde, B. (2019). Smiling for negotiating topic transitions in french conversation. In *GESPIN-Gesture and Speech in Interaction*.

Amoyal, M., Priego-Valverde, B., and Rauzy, S. (2020). Paco: A corpus to analyze the impact of common ground in spontaneous face-to-face interaction. In *Language Resources and Evaluation Conference*.

Bavelas, J. B., Coates, L., and Johnson, T. (2000). Listeners as co-narrators. *Journal of personality and social psychology*, 79(6):941.

Bonin, P., Méot, A., and Bugaiska, A. (2018). Concreteness norms for 1,659 french words: Relationships with other psycholinguistic variables and word recognition times. *Behavior research methods*, 50(6):2366–2387.

Boudin, A., Bertrand, R., Rauzy, S., Ochs, M., and Blache, P. (2021). A multimodal model for predicting conversational feedbacks. In *International Conference on Text, Speech, and Dialogue*, pages 537–549. Springer.

Brunner, L. J. (1979). Smiles can be back channels. *Journal of personality and social psychology*, 37(5):728.

Duncan, S., Brunner, L. J., and Fiske, D. W. (1979). Strategy signals in face-to-face interaction. *Journal of Personality and Social Psychology*, 37(2):301.

El Haddad, K., Çakmak, H., Gilmartin, E., Dupont, S., and Dutoit, T. (2016). Towards a listening agent: A system generating audiovisual laughs and smiles to show interest. In *Proceedings of the 18th ACM International Conference on Multimodal Interaction*, ICMI '16, page 248–255, New York, NY, USA. Association for Computing Machinery.

Gironzetti, E., Attardo, S., and Pickering, L. (2016). Smiling, gaze, and humor in conversation: A pilot study. In Leonor Ruiz-Gurillo, editor, *Metapragmatics of Humor: Current research trends*, pages 235 – 254.

Glas, N. and Pelachaud, C. (2015). Definitions of engagement in human-agent interaction. In *2015 International Conference on Affective Computing and Intelligent Interaction (ACII)*, pages 944–949. IEEE.

Heerey, E. A. and Crossley, H. M. (2013). Predictive and reactive mechanisms in smile reciprocity. *Psychological Science*, 24(8):1446–1455.

Hoque, M., Morency, L.-P., and Picard, R. W. (2011). Are you friendly or just polite?–analysis of smiles in spontaneous face-to-face interactions. In *International Conference on Affective Computing and Intelligent Interaction*, pages 135–144. Springer.

Horton, W. S. (2017). Theories and approaches to the study of conversation and interactive discourse. In *The Routledge handbook of discourse processes*, pages 22–68. Routledge.

Jensen, M. (2015). Smile as feedback expressions in interpersonal interaction. *International Journal of Psychological Studies*, 7(4):95–105.

Kok, I. d. and Heylen, D. (2011). When do we smile? analysis and modeling of the nonverbal context of listener smiles in conversation. In *International Conference on Affective Computing and Intelligent Interaction*, pages 477–486. Springer.

Mazzocconi, C., Tian, Y., and Ginzburg, J. (2020). What's your laughter doing there? a taxonomy of the pragmatic functions of laughter. *IEEE Transactions on Affective Computing*, pages 1–1.

Pickering, M. J. and Garrod, S. (2013). An integrated theory of language production and comprehension. *Behavioral and brain sciences*, 36(4):329–347.

Priego-Valverde, B., Bigi, B., and Amoyal, M. (2020). "cheese!": a corpus of face-to-face french interactions. a case study for analyzing smiling and conversational humor. In *Proceedings of the 12th Language Resources and Evaluation Conference*, pages 467–475.

Rauzy, S. and Amoyal, M. (2020). SMAD: a tool for automatically annotating the smile intensity along a video record. In *HRC2020, 10th Humour Research Conference*.

Rauzy, S., Montcheuil, G., and Blache, P. (2014). Marsatag, a tagger for french written texts and speech transcriptions. In *Second Asian Pacific Corpus linguistics Conference*, pages 220–220.

Rauzy, S., Amoyal, M., and Priego-Valverde, B. (2022). A measure of the smiling synchrony in the conversational face-to-face interaction corpus PACO-CHEESE. In *SmiLa Workshop, Language Resources and Evaluation Conference*.

Schegloff, E. A. (1982). Discourse as an interactional achievement: Some uses of 'uh huh'and other things that come between sentences. *Analyzing discourse: Text and talk*, 71:71–93.

Tolins, J. and Tree, J. E. F. (2014). Addressee backchannels steer narrative development. *Journal of Pragmatics*, 70:152–164.

Proceedings of the Smiling and Laughter across Contexts and the Life-span Workshop @LREC2022, pages 11–15
Marseille, 24 June 2022

Gender Differences, Smiling, and Economic Negotiation Outcomes

Paulina Hiersch, Gary McKeown, Ioana Latu, Magdalena Rychlowska
University of Vienna, Queen's University Belfast, Queen's University Belfast, Queen's University Belfast,
Universitätsring 1, 1010 Wien, Austria, David Keir Bldg, 18-30 Malone Rd, Belfast BT9 5BN, United Kingdom
paulina@hauck-hiersch.de, {g.mckeown, i.latu, m.rychlowska}@qub.ac.uk

Abstract

Research documents gender differences in nonverbal behavior and negotiation outcomes. Women tend to smile more often than men and men generally perform better in economic negotiation contexts. Among nonverbal behaviors, smiling can serve various social functions, from rewarding or appeasing others to conveying dominance, and could therefore be extremely useful in economic negotiations. However, smiling has hardly been studied in negotiation contexts. Here we examine links between smiling, gender, and negotiation outcomes. We analyze a corpus of video recordings of participant dyads during mock salary negotiations and test whether women smile more than men and if the amount of smiling can predict economic negotiation outcomes. Consistent with existing literature, women smiled more than men. There was no significant relationship between smiling and negotiation outcomes and gender did not predict negotiation performance. Exploratory analyses showed that expected negotiation outcomes, strongly correlated with actual outcomes, tended to be higher for men than for women. Implications for the gender pay gap and future research are discussed.

Keywords: smile, gender, negotiation

1. Introduction

A smile can say more than a thousand words. But what does it say about women, who tend to smile more often than men (Fischer and LaFrance, 2015; LaFrance et al., 2003)? Smiling is a powerful interactional signal with multiple functions, which can include rewarding another person, appeasing someone, or negotiating social hierarchies (Martin et al., 2017). However, little is known about the effects of smiles in economic negotiation and about the extent to which such effects are influenced by gender.

In general, women perform worse in negotiations than men (Mazei et al., 2015; Stuhlmacher and Walters, 1999), which is one of the explanations for the gender pay gap. In the European Union, women still earn on average 14.1% less than men (European Commission, 2018) and in the United Kingdom this number is as high as 15.5% (Office for National Statistics, 2020). Although the gender pay gap is likely influenced by various factors such as women's career choices and gender-based discrimination, examining women's performance in economic negotiations can provide further insights into the complexity of gender discrepancies in salaries.

Women's negotiation performance as well as their nonverbal behaviors have been interpreted in the light of power differences between the sexes (e.g., Henley, 1977; Miles and Clenney, 2010). In absence of other cues, men tend to be ascribed a higher social status then women (e.g., Dovidio et al., 1988). People with a higher status benefit from a higher perceived legitimacy of their actions (Amantullah and Tinsley, 2013) and can use a broader repertoire of behaviors without being exposed to social backlash (Rudman, 1998). As a consequence, men might be advantaged in bargaining situations as they are expected to be more competent. Conversely, women might be perceived as less competent and expected to perform less well in negotiations, which might turn into a self-fulfilling prophecy and influence women's verbal and nonverbal behavior during negotiation (Miles and Clenney, 2010). Smiling can be one of such behaviors. Specifically, because of their lower social status, women may smile more often than men to meet social expectations, relieve social tension, comply, and appease (Henley, 1977). Men, benefitting from a higher social status, may feel less pressured to adhere to similar display rules for smiling.

Although gender differences in status, negotiation performance, and nonverbal behavior including smiling have been extensively investigated in previous research, they also tend to be examined separately, and studies that jointly examine these variables are scarce (Hall, 2006; Dovidio et al., 1988). The goal of the present research is to examine how gender, status, and the amount of smiling influence bargaining outcomes during mock salary negotiations. As mentioned earlier, metanalyses show that negotiation outcomes are worse for women than for men (Mazei et al., 2015; Stuhlmacher and Walters, 1999), often leaving women at disadvantage regarding salaries, bonuses, or mortgage payments. However, this effect can be affected by many moderators. For example, women are more effective at the bargaining table when they negotiate on behalf of someone else, when they are more experienced, and when the situation and the potential outcomes are clearly structured (Mazei et al., 2015). Status and power also matter: When reminded of a past experience in which they felt powerful, women negotiate as well as men (Hong and van der Wijst, 2013). Having a higher status, as indicated by a higher organizational rank, can also reduce or eliminate gender differences (Amantullah and Tinsley, 2013). This effect can be explained by social role theory (Eagly, 1987) and status characteristics theory (Berger et al., 1977). According to both theories, assuming a specific social position creates expectations that influence the behavior of the person in this role. Although people automatically associate men with more powerful positions when no other cues are available (Miles and Clenney, 2010), manipulations related to power and status have the potential to improve women's negotiation performance.

This claim is supported by a recent study conducted by Pardal and colleagues (2020). Upon arrival, male and female participants underwent a sequential priming task as a measure of implicit gender stereotypes and were asked to estimate the percentage of men and women who are strong negotiators in the workplace to measure explicit stereotypes. They were then paired with another person and invited to conduct a mock negotiation in the context of an employment contract for the position of a marketing manager. Participants were randomly assigned to play the role of the recruiter (higher social status) or the candidate (lower social status). During the negotiation, both participants received points for each item that they agreed on. Items included the salary, the signing bonus, vacation days, or the work location. The sum of points that each participant received served as a measure of their negotiation performance. All sessions were videotaped. The subsequent analysis revealed that women's negotiation performance was influenced by their role, the gender of their counterpart, and their counterpart's implicit and explicit stereotypes. Specifically, female candidates (lower status) performed significantly worse when their counterpart was male and high in implicit stereotypes. Conversely, female recruiters' (higher status) performance was lowest when their counterpart was lowest and held low explicit but high implicit stereotypes. These findings suggest that implicit biases have an important effect on women's performance at the bargaining table. They also highlight the importance of social status as a potential moderator of this relationship.

Although Pardal and colleagues (2020) collected rich audiovisual material on verbal and nonverbal behaviors during mock negotiations, this material was not analyzed up to date. An exploration of facial expressions, gestures and bodily postures during this study could provide insights into gender differences in negotiation outcomes. Implicit stereotypes are closely linked with nonverbal behavior (Dovidio et al., 2002). It is thus possible that participants' own, and their counterparts' biases influenced participants' nonverbal communication thereby shaping their negotiation performance. Such an interpretation dovetails with extant research showing that social status can be communicated via smiling and laughter. For example, Oveis and colleagues (2016) showed that powerful individuals laugh differently than those with less power, and that listeners are able to recognize this difference and assign social status accordingly. Smiles and laughs have also been described as flexible social signals serving to communicate reward, affiliation (or appeasement), and dominance (Martin et al., 2017) and it is possible that functions and forms of smiles covary with status. For example, subordination theory (Henley, 1977) argues that low-status individuals smile more than high-status individuals as a gesture of appeasement, theoretically congruent with the affiliative functions of smiles. Conversely, dominance smiles could be more frequent among high-status individuals. Up to date, findings on smiling and status are mixed, and it is unclear whether people smile more when they have more power or when they have less power (Cashdan, 1998; Dovidio et al., 1988; Hall, 2006; Hecht and LaFrance, 1998; Ketelaar et al., 2012).

Considerations of gender further complexify the picture, given that display rules for emotion expressions and gender role expectations are different for men and women. Specifically, men are more readily associated with anger and women are more associated with happiness and smiling (Becker, 2007). Men are also expected to feel and express emotions associated with power and competence, whereas women are stereotyped to display powerless emotions such as fear, sadness, and shame (Fischer and Evers, 2011; Fisher et al., 2013). Women who smile are perceived as more attractive whereas the opposite is true for men (Tracy and Beall, 2011).

In addition to being stereotyped as more likely to smile, women have indeed been found to smile and laugh more than men (Fischer and LaFrance, 2015, LaFrance et al., 2003). Importantly, this effect is moderated by power and status. For example, Hecht and LaFrance (1998) found that differences in smiling between men and women were more pronounced in contexts of equal power than in the context of a job interview involving a power discrepancy. However, a later meta-analysis performed by the same research team (LaFrance et al., 2003) points in the opposite direction. Specifically, gender differences in smiling tend to be reduced when women and men hold a similar status – for example, both are in a high position such as being the boss or the teacher, or when both are in a low position such as being the employee or the student.

Gender, status, and smiling appear to be closely linked. Smiling is more frequent among women and can be used to convey status or to negotiate social hierarchies. Thus, it may play an important role in bargaining situations, potentially influencing negotiation performance and outcomes. For this reason, the present study focuses on the role of smiling during negotiations and its relationship with gender and status. Specifically, we investigate how gender, status, and smiling affect negotiation outcomes. For this purpose, we analyze the recordings of mock salary negotiations from the study by Pardal and colleagues (2020), with a specific focus on gender, negotiation status (recruiter versus candidate), and the amount of smiling as potential predictors of negotiation outcomes. Exploratory analyses examined the ideal negotiation outcome reported by participants prior to the negotiation task.

We expected to replicate metanalytic findings that women smile more (Hypothesis 1), and that negotiation outcomes would be worse for women than for men (Hypothesis 2). We also examined whether the amount of smiling would be negatively correlated with negotiation performance (Hypothesis 3), and that negotiation status would not affect men's performance but female recruiters (higher status) would perform better than female candidates (lower status; Hypothesis 4).

2. Method

2.1 Participants

Subjects (N = 144, 40 male, 104 female) were students at an introductory psychology course at a U.S. university (Pardal et al., 2020). The collected data involved 72 dyads (46 same-gender, 26 mixed). However, videos of two participants were partly missing and 17 participants had to be excluded from further analyses either because their faces were not fully visible on the recordings, because of missing data, or because the dyad did not reach an agreement in the negotiation task. The final sample included data from 125 participants (32 male, 93 female).

2.2 Procedure

Details of the experiment are described in Pardal et al. (2020). Upon arrival, participants were informed that they would be participating in two different studies. The two parts of the study were completed in different rooms. In the first part of the study, participants completed a sequential priming task designed to measure implicit gender-negotiation stereotypes and a short survey assessing explicit stereotypes. These measures are outside of the scope of the present study and will not be discussed further.

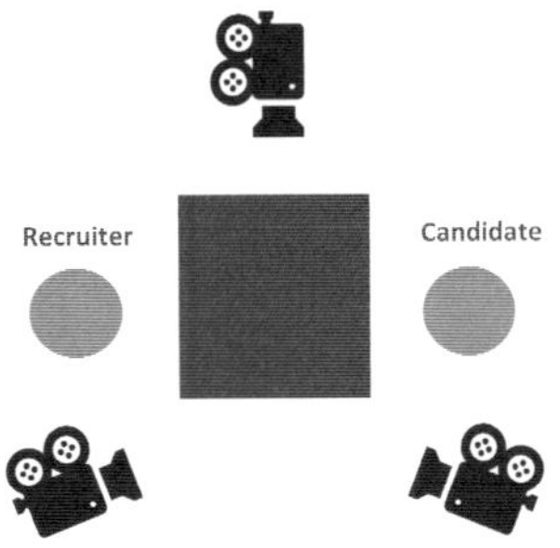

Figure 1: Layout of a negotiation session.

Participants then moved to another laboratory designed to look like a boardroom. They were matched with another person and invited to take part in a mock negotiation of an employment contract. Participants were then randomly assigned the role of either recruiter or candidate, a manipulation designed to operationalize social status. The candidate has just been hired as a marketing manager and was to negotiate for salary, signing bonus, vacation days, and location. Conversely, the recruiter has just hired the candidate and was instructed to negotiate in the interest of their company. Both participants were instructed to earn as many points as possible according to a specific matrix that they were advised not to share with one another. The matrix assigned a specific number of points to each possible outcome depending on the negotiation role. The dyad was then allowed 10 min to prepare the strategy. Right before starting the negotiation, participants reported their ideal negotiation outcome. The negotiation session was videotaped and Figure 1 displays the experimental setting. The task ended once the participants reached an agreement and signed a fictitious employment contract.

2.3 Measures

2.3.1 Actual and Ideal Negotiation Performance

Negotiation performance was operationalized by the sum of points that each participant received across the four negotiated items: salary, signing bonus, vacation days, and location. The outcome ranged from 0 to 2000 points for each person. The same range applied for the ideal negotiation outcome, reported by participants prior to the actual negotiation task.

2.3.2 Amount of Smiling

We used the software ELAN (Version 6.3, 2021, see Figure 2) to manually annotate smiling for each participant during the actual negotiation task. Annotations started when the experimenter left the room or when they explicitly told participants that the negotiation could begin. The end of negotiation was signaled with a handshake, by a verbal agreement, or by signing the contract.

After determining the beginning and the end of the negotiation for each dyad, the recording of this task was divided into 400ms intervals. For each of these intervals, we determined the intensity of smiling using a scale ranging from Level 0 (neutral, no smile) to Level 4 (most intense open-mouth smile), according to the procedure described by Gironzetti and colleagues (2016) and based on the Facial Action Coding System (FACS, Ekman and Friesen, 1978). Figure 3 represents different levels of smile intensity annotated coding scheme. The present research focuses on the amount of smiling for each participant. To create a metric of how much recruiters and candidates smiled during the negotiation task, we divided, for each individual, the number of intervals with values higher than 0 (indicating the presence of a smile) by the total number of intervals comprising the task. This variable, henceforth named smiling score, represents the proportion of time that each participant spent smiling during the negotiation task.

Figure 2: Annotating smiles in ELAN.

In cases where participants' mouth or faces were covered (e.g., by a paper, their own head, or their negotiation partner) and when it was not possible to confidently determine whether they were smiling or not, the corresponding intervals were excluded from the calculation of the smiling score.

3. Results

Measures of negotiation performance and smiling were used to investigate how gender and negotiation role influence smiling and negotiation outcomes. On average, participants smiled during 44.53% of the negotiation task ($SD = 0.24$) and reached an average negotiation outcome of 1231.44 points ($SD = 371.15$).

We first examined how much time male and female participants spent smiling. Consistent with Hypothesis 1, women smiled more than men (M = 47.17% of session time, $SD = 0.25$ vs. $M = 37.41\%$, $SD = 0.19$, respectively). A subsequent Welch's ANOVA showed that this difference was statistically significant, $F(1,70) = 5.47$, $p = .022$.

In line with the existing literature on the gender gap and men's and women's negotiation skills, we expected that, compared to male participants, women would earn less points in the negotiation task (Hypothesis 2). However, the number of points earned by men was only slightly higher than the number of points earned by women ($M = 1271.31$, $SD = 318.82$ vs. $M = 1217.71$, $SD = 389.46$), and this difference was not statistically significant, $F(1, 65) = 0.597$, $p = .442$.

Hypothesis 3 predicted that, for female participants, the amount of smiling would be associated with lower negotiation outcomes. We examined correlations between the smiling score and the negotiation outcomes separately for both genders. Neither of the two correlations was significant , $r(91) = .026$, $p = .807$ for female participants

Level 0 *Level 1* *Level 2* *Level 3* *Level 4*

Figure 3 : Different levels of smile intensity and the corresponding annotations.

and $r(30) = .001$, $p = .995$ for male participants.

Finally, Hypothesis 4 predicted that the negotiation role, manipulated as a proxy for social status would affect women's, but not men's negotiation performance. Specifically, we expected female recruiters, assigned a higher-status role, to perform better than female candidates, who negotiated in a lower-status role. This hypothesis was not supported by the data: an analysis of variance examining negotiation outcomes as a function of negotiation role, gender, and their interaction revealed no significant interaction effect, $F(1,121) = 1.948$, $p = .165$. The main effect of negotiation role and the main effect of gender were also not significant, $F(1,121) = 1.292$, $p = .258$, and $F(1,121) = 1.122$, $p = .148$, respectively.

In addition to testing Hypotheses 1-4, we explored the ideal negotiation outcome reported by participants prior to the main negotiation task. This measure was significantly and positively correlated with the actual negotiation outcome, $r(120) = .725$, $p < .001$. Ideal negotiation outcome also tended to be lower among women ($M = 1116.48$, $SD = 377.72$) than men ($M = 1233.87$, $SD = 299.27$), but failed to reach conventional levels of significance, $F(1,65) = 3.092$, $p = 0.083$.

4. Discussion

The aim of the current study was to examine how nonverbal communication, in particular smiling, contributes to men's and women's performance in economic negotiations. We analyzed a corpus of video recordings of mock salary negotiations collected for the needs of a previous study (Pardal et al., 2020). In addition to examining how gender and negotiation status influenced participants' negotiation outcomes, we annotated and measured the amount of smiling displayed by male and female participants.

Our analyses showed that women smiled more than men. This finding is congruent with a large body of evidence showing that women are expected to smile more than men (e.g., Becker, 2007; Tracy and Beall, 2011) and that they indeed smile and laugh more frequently than their male counterparts (Fischer and LaFrance, 2015; LaFrance et al. 2003).

The amount of smiling did not predict negotiation outcomes, neither for female nor for male participants. Although this finding may appear surprising, it dovetails with somewhat mixed results on smiling in interaction. Although smiling people are perceived as competent, dominant, and having a high social status (e.g., Knutson, 1996; Senior et al., 1999), smiles are also displayed when expressers are uncomfortable (e.g., Ekman et al., 1988). In such contexts, smiles may serve to mask negative feelings or to meet social norms. Women are often expected to smile and are portrayed to be more affiliative than men (Hess et al., 2005). Functions and forms of smiles vary, with some smiles expressing happiness, and others appeasement or dominance (Martin et al., 2017). It is thus possible that the mere quantification of the amount of smiling does not reflect the complexity of smiles displayed during mock negotiation. Future research should include more nuanced measures of smiling, such as the patterns of smiling, smiling intensity, or types of smiles (Martin et al., 2017). Another possibility is that, given the relatively artificial setting of the mock negotiation task used in the present research, participants mostly displayed polite smiles to acknowledge their counterparts or to mask feelings of awkwardness. Future analyses of this dataset could examine the form of smiles displayed by participants and combine it with measures of participants' engagement in the negotiation task – for example time of the negotiation or the amount of conversations between the recruiter and the candidate.

Unexpectedly, women's negotiation outcomes were comparable to men's. It is possible that through negotiation training and societal changes in the last years, women have already been able to enhance their skills. However, it is also important to note that our negotiation task did not use real-life incentives and our sample consisted of students with little or no experience in negotiating, thereby limiting the generalizability of our results. The instructions of the task and its design to assign point values were designed to motivate and engage participants to behave as closely as possible to their assigned roles. Nevertheless, behaviors may differ in real-life settings. Another limitation is that our sample included 104 women and only 40 men, potentially lacking power for meaningful comparisons between the two genders (Simmons et al., 2018). Finally, neither the negotiation role nor the interaction between negotiation role and gender did influence participant's outcomes. Additional measures of the extent to which the recruiter and the candidate felt powerful – or were perceived as such – could provide more insights into this null finding.

Finally, our results suggest that, compared to men, women tend to expect less from their negotiations. Given that expected negotiation outcome is strongly and positively correlated with the actual outcomes, low expectations could act as self-fulfilling prophecies and negatively affect their bargaining performance. Future research should include measures of negotiation expectations to further explore this potential connection.

To summarize, we show that, in a mock negotiation task, women smile more than men and they tend to have lower expectations about their negotiation performance, a measure which is correlated with the actual negotiation outcomes. The present report documents first steps of the research project. Further analyses will examine the effects of gender, negotiation role, status, and dyad composition using the Actor-Partner Interdependence Model (Cook and Kenny, 2005), a statistical framework more appropriate for dyadic data. Another analysis of interest focuses on the relationship between gender, smile synchrony, and negotiation outcomes.

5. Bibliographical References

Amanatullah, E. T., & Tinsley, C. H. (2013). Ask and ye shall receive? How gender and status moderate negotiation success. Negotiation and conflict management research, 6(4): 253–272.

Becker, D. V., Kenrick, D. T., Neuberg, S. L., Blackwell, K. C., & Smith, D. M. (2007). The confounded nature of angry men and happy women. *Journal of Personality and Social Psychology, 92*(2): 179–190.

Berger, J., Fisek, M. H., Norman, R. Z., & Zelditch, M. (1977). Status characteristics and social interaction: An expected states approach. New York, NY: Elsevier.

Cashdan, E. (1998). Smiles, speech, and body posture: How women and men display sociometric status and power. *Journal of Nonverbal Behavior, 22*(4): 209–228.

Cook, W. L., & Kenny, D. A. (2005). The actor-partner interdependence model: A model of bidirectional effects in developmental studies. *International Journal of Behavioral Development*, 29: 101–109.

Dovidio, J. F., Heltman, K., Keating, C. F., Brown, C. E., & Ellyson, S. L. (1988). Power displays between women and men in discussions of gender-linked tasks: A multichannel study. *Journal of Personality and Social Psychology,* 55 (4):580–587.

Dovidio, J., Kawakami, K., & Gaertner, S. (2002). Implicit and explicit prejudice and interracial interaction. *Journal of Personality And Social Psychology*, *82*(1), 62–68. https://doi.org/10.1037/0022-3514.82.1.62

Eagly, A. H. (1987). Sex differences in social behavior: A social-role interpretation. Hillsdale, NJ: Erlbaum.

Ekman, P., Friesen, W., & O'Sullivan, M. (1988). Smiles when lying. *Journal of Personality and Social Psychology*, 54(3): 414-420.

ELAN (Version 6.3) [Computer software]. (2022). Nijmegen: Max Planck Institute for Psycholinguistics, The Language Archive. Retrieved from https://archive.mpi.nl/tla/elan

Fischer, A. H., & Evers, C. (2011). The social costs and benefits of anger as a function of gender and relationship context. *Sex Roles*, 65: 23–34.

Fischer, A., & LaFrance, M. (2015). What drives the smile and the tear: Why women are more emotionally expressive than men. *Emotion Review,* 7:22–9.

Gironzetti, E., S. Attardo, & L. Pickering (2016). Smiling, Gaze, and Humor in Conversation: A Pilot Study. In Ruiz-Gurillo, L. (ed.), *Metapragmatics of Humor: Current Research Trends* (235–254). Amsterdam: John Benjamins.

Hall, J.A. (2006). Nonverbal behavior, status, and gender: How do we understand their relations? *Psychology of Women Quarterly,* 30: 384–391.

Hecht, M. A., & LaFrance, M. (1998). License or obligation to smile: The effect of power and sex on amount and type of smiling. *Personality & Social Psychology Bulletin, 24*(12): 1332–1342.

Henley, N. M. (1977). Body politics: Power, sex, and nonverbal communication. Englewood Cliffs, NJ: Prentice-Hall.

Hess, U., Adams, R., & Kleck, R. (2005). Who may frown and who should smile? Dominance, affiliation, and the display of happiness and anger. *Cognition & Emotion*, 19(4): 515–536.

Hong, A.P.C.I, & Van der Wijst, P.J. (2013). Women in negotiation: Effects of gender and power on negotiation behavior. *Negotiation and Conflict Management Research*, 6(4): 273–284.

Ketelaar, T., Koenig, B. L., Gambacorta, D., Dolgov, I., Hor, D., Zarzosa, J., Cuauhtémoc L.-N., Klungle, M., & Wells, L. (2012). Smiles as signals of lower status in football players and fashion models: Evidence that smiles are associated with lower dominance and lower prestige. *Evolutionary Psychology*, 10(3): 371–397.

Knutson, B. (1996). Facial expressions of emotion influence interpersonal trait inferences. *Journal of Nonverbal Behavior*, 20(3): 165–182.

LaFrance, M. Hecht, M.A., & Paluck, E.L. (2003). The contingent smile: A meta-analysis of sex differences in smiling. *Psychological Bulletin*, 2:305–334.

Martin, J., Rychlowska, M., Wood, A., & Niedenthal, P. (2017). Smiles as multipurpose social signals. *Trends In Cognitive Sciences*, *21*(11): 864–877.

Mazei, J., Hüffmeier, J., Freund, P. A., Stuhlmacher, A. F., Bilke, L., & Hertel, G. (2015). A meta-analysis on gender differences in negotiation outcomes and their moderators. *Psychological Bulletin*, 141: 85–104.

Miles, E.W., & Clenney, E. F. (2010). Gender differences in negotiation: A status characteristics theory view. *Negotiation and Conflict Management Research*, 3: 130–144.

Oveis, C., Spectre, A., Smith, P. K., Liu, M. Y., & Keltner, D. (2016). Laughter conveys status. *Journal of Experimental Social Psychology, 65*: 109–115.

Pardal, V., Alger, M., & Latu, I. (2020). Implicit and explicit gender stereotypes at the bargaining table: Male counterparts' stereotypes predict women's lower performance in dyadic face-to-face negotiations. *Sex Roles*, 83: 289-302.

Rudman, L. A. (1998). Self-promotion as a risk factor for women: The costs and benefits of counterstereotypical impression management. *Journal of Personality and Social Psychology*, 74: 629–645.

Senior, C., Phillips, M., Barnes, J., & David, A. (1999). An investigation into the perception of dominance from schematic faces: A study using the World-Wide Web. *Behavior Research Methods, Instruments, & Computers*, 31(2): 341–346.

Simmons, J., Nelson, L., & Simonsohn, U. (2018). False-Positive Citations. *Perspectives on Psychological Science*, *13*(2) : 255–259.

Stuhlmacher, A. F., & Walters, A. E. (1999). Gender differences in negotiation outcome: A meta-analysis. *Personnel Psychology*, 52: 653–677.

Tracy, J. L., & Beall, A. T. (2011). Happy guys finish last: The impact of emotion expressions on sexual attraction. *Emotion,* 11(6): 1379–1387.

Proceedings of the Smiling and Laughter across Contexts and the Life-span Workshop @LREC2022, pages 16–20
Marseille, 24 June 2022

A Measure of the Smiling Synchrony in the Conversational Face-to-face Interaction Corpus PACO-CHEESE

Stéphane Rauzy, Mary Amoyal, Béatrice Priego-Valverde
Aix Marseille Université, CNRS, Laboratoire Parole et Langage UMR 7309
5 avenue Pasteur, BP 80975, 13604 Aix-en-Provence, FRANCE
{stephane.rauzy, mary.amoyal, beatrice.priego-valverde}@univ-amu.fr

Abstract

The smiling synchrony of the French audio-video conversational corpora "PACO" and "Cheese!" is investigated. The two corpora merged altogether last 6 hours and are made of 25 face-to-face dyadic interactions annotated following the 5 levels Smiling Intensity Scale proposed by Gironzetti et al. (2016). After introducing new indicators for characterizing synchrony phenomena, we find that almost all the 25 interactions of PACO-CHEESE show a strong and significant smiling synchrony behavior. We investigate in a second step the evolution of the synchrony parameters throughout the interaction. No effect is found and it appears rather that the smiling synchrony is present at the very start of the interaction and remains unchanged throughout the conversation.

Keywords: Synchrony, convergence, smiling behavior, spontaneous interaction, face-to-face audio-video corpus

1. Introduction

It is now well established that participants involved in a conversational face-to-face activity exhibit similar patterns, the phenomenon having received various names including among them accommodation (Giles et al., 1991), entrainment (Brennan and Clark, 1996), alignment (Pickering and Garrod, 2004), convergence (Pardo, 2013), mimicry (Pentland, 2008) and synchrony (Edlund et al., 2009). This interactional behavior have been observed in different domains ranging from lexical adaptation (Brennan and Clark, 1996), pronunciation (Aubanel and Nguyen, 2010), prosodic patterns (De Looze et al., 2011), syntactic structures (Pickering and Ferreira, 2008) to facial expressions (Seibt et al., 2015). Herein we will focus on the synchrony analysis of smiles considered as interactive facial gesture (Bavelas and Gerwing, 2007). Convergence issues will be also examined by exploring the evolution of the synchrony parameters throughout the interaction. The synchrony of smiles and laughter have been previously addressed (Heerey and Crossley, 2013; Gironzetti et al., 2016b; Mui et al., 2018; El Haddad et al., 2019; Arnold and Piotr, 2020)). Our contribution is herein twofold: we first propose some new indicators for measuring synchrony and secondly we analyse the smiling synchrony of the PACO-CHEESE corpus.

2. Measuring synchrony

Synchrony can be essentially defined as the property for the participants to show temporally similar behaviours (Edlund et al., 2009). Various methods for measuring synchrony have been proposed in the literature depending on the timescale at which this similarity takes place. Given a variable observed along the time line (e.g. pitch, speech rate, smile intensity, ...), the Pearson's correlation between the two participant's time series is for example a popular indicator of synchrony (Edlund et al., 2009; De Looze and Rauzy, 2011; De Looze et al., 2014). If the match between the two series is not instantaneous but rather presents some time shift, Time-Lagged Cross Correlation techniques can be applied with benefits (Golland et al., 2019). For more complex time dependencies, alternative measurements relying on cross-spectral and relative phase approaches (Schmidt et al., 2012), mimicry detection (Feese et al., 2012; El Haddad et al., 2019) or cross-recurrence quantification analysis (Main et al., 2016; Paxton and Dale, 2017) have been build up.

In De Looze and Rauzy (2011), the description of synchrony phenomena was tackled by drawing an analogy with the coupled oscillators model found in Physics. The model describes the dynamics of two oscillators (say two pendulums) coupled together by a spring. The spring plays here the role of a force coupling the respective oscillating trajectory x_1 and x_2 of the two pendulum masses. The general solution of the problem let emerge two oscillating *normal modes* associated with the sum and the difference of the trajectories:

$$x_{\text{sum}} = x_1 + x_2 \quad ; \quad x_{\text{diff}} = x_1 - x_2 \qquad (1)$$

The symmetric mode x_{sum} describes the motion of the system as a whole and is characterized by an oscillatory period T_{sum} determined by the two pendulum periods in absence of coupling. The asymmetric mode x_{diff} accounts for the internal oscillations of the two pendulums system and its characteristic period T_{diff} is necessarily shorter than T_{sum} if the system is coupled. This remark leads us to define a *coupling factor* k_c as:

$$k_c = \log(T_{\text{sum}}/T_{\text{diff}}) \quad ; \quad k_c > 0 \Longrightarrow \text{Coupling} \quad (2)$$

This criterion allows in practice to detect the presence of a coupling between the two participants.

The dynamics of the coupled system is determined by a linear combination of the two oscillatory normal modes. It accounts for various coupling behaviours depending on the value of the amplitudes A_{sum} and A_{diff}

respectively associated with the symmetric and asymmetric modes. Pure synchrony corresponds for example to the case $A_{\text{diff}} = 0$ (i.e. $x_1 = x_2$) whereas $A_{\text{sum}} = 0$ depicts the situation of pure anti-synchrony (i.e. the pendulums are forced to move in the opposite direction). The degree of synchrony can be measured by evaluating the *coefficient of synchrony* ρ_S:

$$\rho_S = \frac{var(x_{\text{sum}}) - var(x_{\text{diff}})}{var(x_{\text{sum}}) + var(x_{\text{diff}})} \quad (3)$$

where the variance of the oscillating time series $var(x)$ is proportional to the square of its amplitude (e.g. $var(x_{\text{sum}}) \propto A^2_{\text{sum}}$). The coefficient of synchrony ρ_S varies from -1 to 1 and is indeed close to the Pearson's correlation coefficient $\rho(x_1, x_2)$ of the two observed participant's time series.

Estimation of the periods T_{diff} and T_{sum}

We denote by $W(t; x, \tau)$ the smoothed version of the time series $x \equiv x(t)$ smoothed at time scale τ. For example $W(t; x, \tau)$ can be the result of a Simple Moving Average operation with a window of size τ. Smoothing works herein as a low pass filter which removes from the signal fluctuations with frequency higher than the cut-off frequency. The variance $var(W(t; x, \tau))$, which measures the energy of the smoothed time series, varies from $var(x)$ when $\tau = 0$ (since $W(t; x, \tau = 0) \equiv x(t)$) to 0 when τ approaches infinity (in practice when τ is greater that the largest fluctuation present in the signal). We define the quantity $F(x, \tau)$ as the ratio of energy contained in the fluctuations with characteristic time scale lower than the smoothing time scale τ:

$$F(x, \tau) = 1 - \frac{var(W(t; x, \tau))}{var(x)} \quad (4)$$

The ratio $F(x, \tau)$ varies from 0 at time scale $\tau = 0$ and approaches 1 when τ is large enough. It represents the cumulative distribution function of the energy up to the time scale τ. The energy contained between two time scales τ_{inf} and τ_{sup} is given by $E(\tau_{\text{inf}}, \tau_{\text{sup}}) = F(x, \tau_{\text{sup}}) - F(x, \tau_{\text{inf}})$ and the energy density can be obtained by differentiating the cumulative energy distribution $F(x, \tau)$.

The characteristic periods T_{diff} and T_{sum} associated with the two oscillating modes of the coupled system will be estimated from the energy distribution function of the two series. One can choose for example the time scale corresponding to the maximal peak of energy density as the characteristic period of the mode. The choice of the appropriate estimator will eventually depends on the form of the energy distribution function.

3. The PACO-CHEESE corpus

The PACO-CHEESE corpus results of the merge of the two French audio-video conversational corpora "PACO" (Amoyal et al., 2020) and "Cheese!" (Priego-Valverde et al., 2020; Priego-Valverde et al., 2018). The "Cheese!" corpus is composed of 11 dyadic interactions lasting between 15 to 20 minutes each. The two participants were recorded in an anechoic room with separate microphone and camera. The participants were asked to read each other a canned joke before freely conversing during the rest of the interaction. The corpus "PACO" contains 15 conversations and has been collected by following the same protocol as designed for "Cheese!". The main contrast between the two corpora is that the "Cheese!" participants were acquainted since they were students in the same class whereas "PACO" participants did not know each other. This condition is intended in practice to control the relationship factor between the two interlocutors (i.e. "acquainted" vs "initial interaction").

The smile intensity annotations

Smiles have been annotated thanks to the "Smiling Intensity Scale" (SIS) (Gironzetti et al., 2016a). The 5 levels of the scale start with level 0 (neutral face), contain three gradual intensities of smile (from 1 to 3) and end with level 4 encoding laughter. Each smile intensity category involves a specific combination of Action Units (AUs) detailed by the Facial Action Coding System (FACS) (Ekman and Friesen, 1978). The full description of the annotation procedure as well as a discussion concerning the benefits to adopt the 5 levels SIS system can be found in (Amoyal et al., 2020; Rauzy and Amoyal, 2020).

4. The smiling synchrony in PACO-CHEESE

4.1. Global synchrony

We investigate in this section the global smiling synchrony at the scale of the interaction for the 25 conversations of the PACO-CHEESE corpus. The starting canned jokes passage (see section 3) have been removed by cutting the first 3 minutes of each conversation.

For each interaction, the two times series x_1 and x_2 of the participants are extracted according to the smile intensity annotations presented section 3. The sum and the difference mentioned equation 1 are formed. An illustration of the trajectories of the 4 time series is presented figure 1.

The characteristic periods T_{sum} and T_{diff} are afterwards estimated. The top panel of figure 2 shows for the 4 time series the cumulative distribution function (CDF) of energy as defined equation 4. For the diad named ACMZ, the x_1, x_2 and x_{sum} present similar CDFs, with a median time scale around 9 seconds. The energy CDF of the asymmetric mode x_{diff} is by contrast shifted towards the low timescales (i.e. the median period is around 4 seconds).

A thorough analysis of the 25 PACO-CHEESE interactions reveals that the energy density distribution of the smile time series is well described by a lognormal distribution. The bottom panel of figure 2 presents the fitted lognormal models for the 4 time series of the ACMZ interaction. Our estimates of the characteristic periods T_{sum} and T_{diff} mentioned equation 2 will finally correspond to the peaks of the fitted energy densities for x_{sum} and x_{diff}.

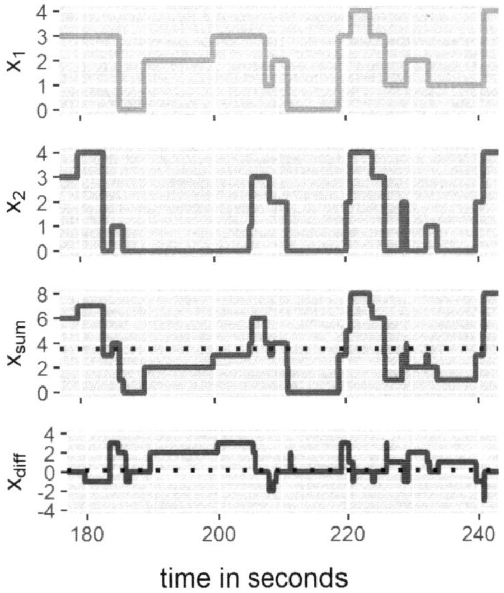

Figure 1: CHEESE-ACMZ interaction: A 60 seconds extract of the smile intensity time series (SIS encoded) for the two participants (panels x_1 and x_2) and their corresponding x_{sum} and x_{diff} variations.

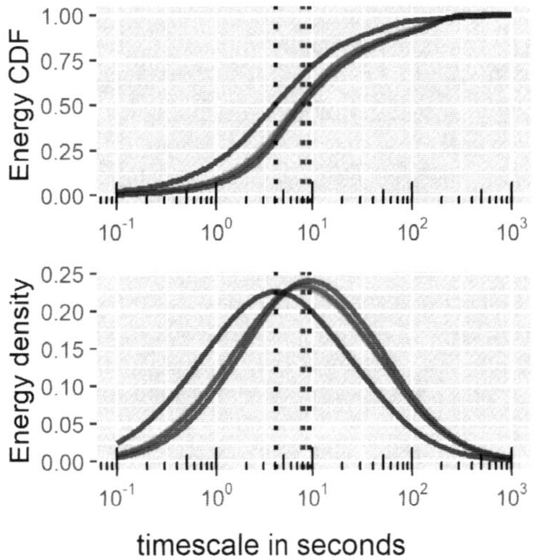

Figure 2: CHEESE-ACMZ interaction: (top panel) the cumulative distribution function of energy for the time series $x1$ (orange), x_2 (green), x_{sum} (red) and x_{diff} (blue) in function of the cut-off timescale (logarithmic scale). (bottom panel) The corresponding energy density models assuming a lognormal energy distribution.

At this stage, we observe that the asymmetric period T_{diff} is half as long as its symmetric counterpart T_{sum}. According to the criterion introduced equation 2, it suggests that the smile intensities of the ACMZ participants are in fact coupled. It remains however to show that this discrepency is statistically significant.

Standard errors associated to the estimates of the periods, the coupling factor k_c and the coefficient of synchrony are obtained by applying a random pairing strategy (Golland et al., 2019). A random pair of participants is created by pairing two participants not belonging to the same interaction. By construction there is no coupling for this fake interaction. Within the uncertainties due to statistical fluctuations, the values estimated from the fake interaction is thus the one expected for the no coupling condition.

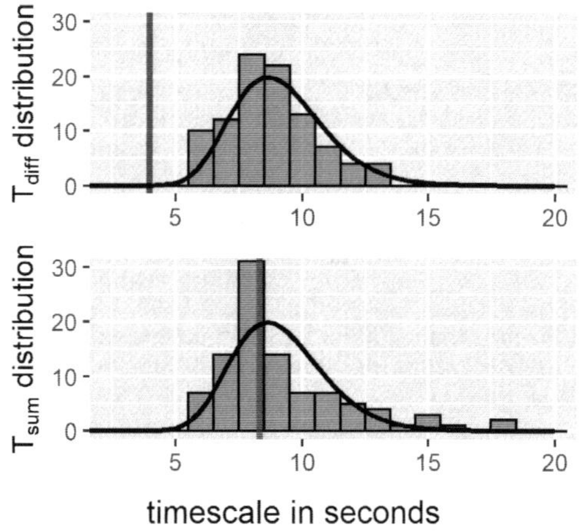

Figure 3: CHEESE-ACMZ interaction: (top panel) Histogram of the T_{diff} period estimate for the 96 random pairs. The black curve is a lognormal density fitted on the histogram distribution. Blue vertical line around 4 s indicates the real T_{diff} for the ACMZ pair. (bottom panel) Same plot for the T_{sum} period estimate.

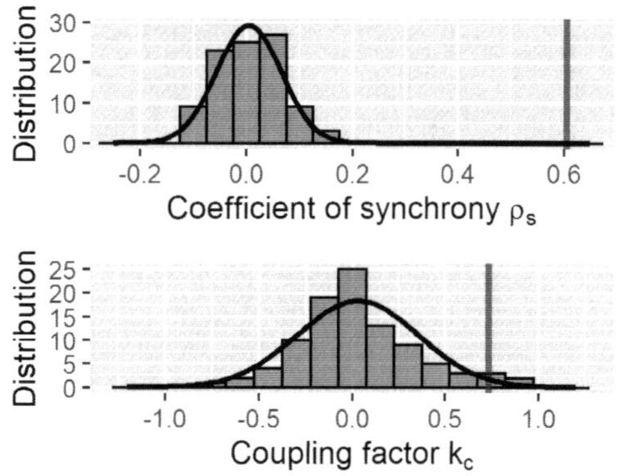

Figure 4: CHEESE-ACMZ interaction: Same plot as in figure 3 for the estimate of the coefficient of synchrony ρ_S (top panel) and the coupling factor k_C (bottom panel).

For each of the 25 interactions of the PACO-CHEESE corpus, we formed the 2x48 random pairs and computed for each pair the parameter estimates. The results are illustrated figures 3 and 4 for the ACMZ interaction. The distribution of the estimates for the random pairs allows to compute the standard deviation associated with the estimator and the expected value in the no coupling condition. Figure 3 shows that T_{sum} and

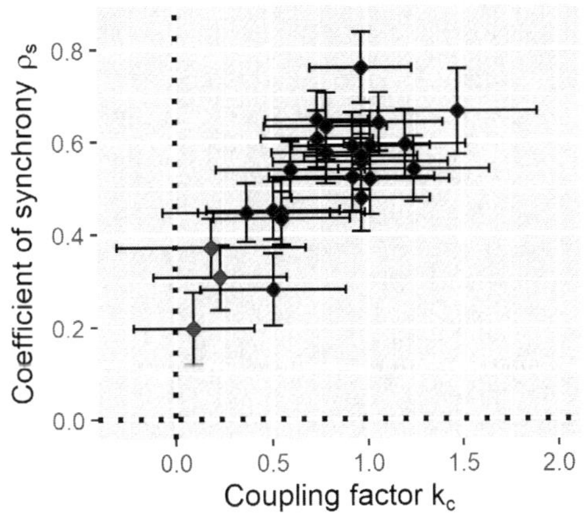

Figure 5: The coefficient of synchrony and the coupling factor for the 25 interactions of the PACO-CHEESE corpus. Red points denote T_{diff} periods greater than 9 seconds.

T_{diff} are expected to be identical in the absence of coupling and that the value of T_{diff} for the real pair AC-MZ (the blue vertical line) is clearly shorter than the one expected by chance. One can also see figure 4 that in absence of coupling the expected values for the coupling factor and the coefficient of synchrony are centered on 0 and that the observed values for the true pair AC-MZ are far above this threshold within the standard deviation.

The final result is presented figure 5 for the 25 interactions. The 1σ error bars are computed for each interaction using the random pairs strategy mentioned above. After removing the 3 outlying interactions with T_{diff} greater than 9 seconds (the red points on the graph), the mean T_{diff} is 5.41 s with a standard dispersion of 1.23 s to compare with 13.65 s and 5.66 s for the T_{sum} period. The mean T_{diff} and T_{max} define respectively timescales below which the participants are locally not aligned and above which the synchrony is observed. For all the interactions of PACO-CHEESE the participants show a strong synchrony in their smiling behaviour, this property is revealed both by the significant measurements of the coupling factor and the coefficient of synchrony.

4.2. Synchrony and evolution

Since smiling synchrony appears as a general behaviour adopted by participants, the question arises whether the synchrony strength evolves throughout the conversation or instead remains constant. We sliced each interaction in 5 time windows of equal duration, from a starting time at 180 seconds to the end of the interaction (the mean bin duration is 182 seconds containing around 30 smile changes in average). Each window bins contains thus several periods of the T_{sum} symmetric mode which warrants in practice the safe evaluation of the synchrony parameters.

Figure 6 illustrates the variation of the synchrony mea-

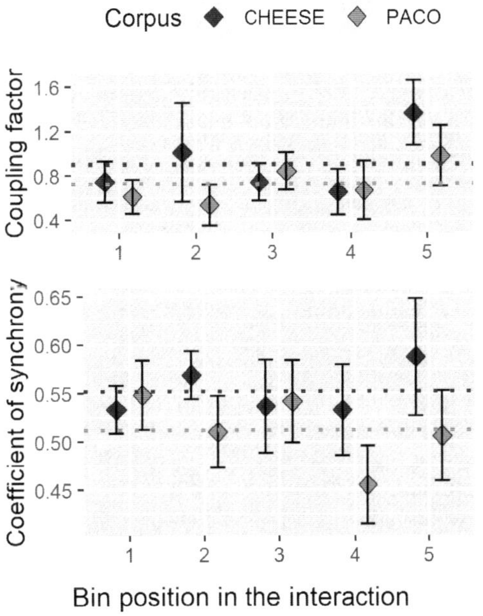

Figure 6: Variation of the synchrony parameters in function of the window bin position in the conversation. The averages and 1σ error bars are computed individually for each corpus (11 interactions for CHEESE and 12 for PACO).

surements throughout the conversation. For each bin position, we computed the averages and 1σ error bars over the interactions of each corpus. The estimates of the coupling factor and the coefficient of synchrony do not reveal any evolution trend. For both corpora, it appears that the smiling synchrony is rather present at the very start of the interaction and remains unchanged throughout the conversation.

5. Conclusions

We performed a synchrony analysis of the smile annotations of the PACO-CHEESE corpus encoded following the Smiling Intensity Scale. We introduced new indicators allowing to define two timescales associated with the synchrony phenomenon, one period around 5 seconds below which participant's smiling are locally not aligned and a second period around 14 seconds above which the similarity between the two smiling behaviors takes place. That period also settles in practice the minimal timescale required to study smiling synchrony. As expected from previous study on face-to-face conversations (Heerey and Crossley, 2013), the results reveal that almost all the 25 interactions of PACO-CHEESE show a strong and significant smiling synchrony behavior. In a second step, the question of the convergence was investigated by measuring the evolution of the synchrony parameters throughout the interaction. We did not found such an effect, the smiling synchrony is indeed detected at the outset of the conversation and its strength does not increase along time.

6. Bibliographical References

Amoyal, M., Priego-Valverde, B., and Rauzy, S. (2020). PACO: A corpus to analyze the impact of common ground in spontaneous face-to-face interaction. In *Language Resources and Evaluation Conference*, Marseille, France, May.

Arnold, A. J. and Piotr, W. (2020). Smile (but only deliberately) though your heart is aching: Loneliness is associated with impaired spontaneous. *Social Neuroscience*.

Aubanel, V. and Nguyen, N. (2010). Automatic recognition of regional phonological variation in conversational interaction. *Speech Communication*, 52:577–586, 06.

Bavelas, J. B. and Gerwing, J. (2007). Conversational hand gestures and facial displays in face-to-face dialogue. *Social communication*, pages 283–308.

Brennan, S. and Clark, H. H. (1996). Conceptual pacts and lexical choice in conversation. *Journal of Experimental Psychology: Learning, Memory and Cognition*, 22:1482–1493.

De Looze, C. and Rauzy, S. (2011). Measuring speakers' similarity in speech by means of prosodic cues: methods and potential. In *Interspeech 2011*, Florence, Italy.

De Looze, C., Oertel, C., Rauzy, S., and Campbell, N. (2011). Measuring dynamics of mimicry by means of prosodic cues in conversational speech. In *ICPhS 2011*, Hong-Kong, China.

De Looze, C., Scherer, S., Vaughan, B., and Campbell, N. (2014). Investigating automatic measurements of prosodic accommodation and its dynamics in social interaction. *Speech Commun.*, 58:11–34, mar.

Edlund, J., Herldner, M., and Hirschberg, J. (2009). Pause and gap length in face-to-face interaction. In *Interspeech*, pages 2779–2782.

Ekman, P. and Friesen, W. V. (1978). *Facial Action Coding System: Manual*, volume vol. 1-2. Consulting Psychologists Press.

El Haddad, K., Chakravarthula, S. N., and Kennedy, J. (2019). Smile and laugh dynamics in naturalistic dyadic interactions: Intensity levels, sequences and roles. In *2019 International Conference on Multimodal Interaction*, pages 259–263. ACM.

Feese, S., Arnrich, B., Tröster, G., Meyer, B., and Jonas, K. (2012). Quantifying behavioral mimicry by automatic detection of nonverbal cues from body motion. In *2012 International Conference on Privacy, Security, Risk and Trust and 2012 International Confernece on Social Computing*, pages 520–525.

Giles, H., Coupland, N., and Coupland, J., (1991). *Accommodation theory: Communication, context, and consequence*, page 1–68. Studies in Emotion and Social Interaction. Cambridge University Press.

Gironzetti, E., Attardo, S., and Pickering, L. (2016a). Smiling, gaze, and humor in conversation: A pilot study. In Leonor Ruiz-Gurillo, editor, *Metapragmatics of Humor: Current research trends*, pages 235 – 254.

Gironzetti, E., Pickering, L., Huang, M., Zhang, Y., Menjo, S., and Attardo, S. (2016b). Smiling synchronicity and gaze patterns in dyadic humorous conversations. *HUMOR*, 29(2):301–324.

Golland, Y., Mevorach, D., and Levit-Binnun, N. (2019). Affiliative zygomatic synchrony in copresent strangers. *Scientific Reports*, 9(1):3120, February.

Heerey, E. A. and Crossley, H. M. (2013). Predictive and reactive mechanisms in smile reciprocity. *Psychological Science*, 24(8):1446–1455.

Main, A., Paxton, A., and Dale, A. (2016). An exploratory analysis of emotion dynamics between mothers and adolescents during conflict discussions. *Emotion*, 16(6):913–928.

Mui, P. H. C., Goudbeek, M. B., Roex, C., Spierts, W., and Swerts, M. G. J. (2018). Smile mimicry and emotional contagion in audio-visual computer-mediated communication. *Frontiers in Psychology*, 9.

Pardo, J. (2013). Measuring phonetic convergence in speech production. *Frontiers in Psychology*, 4.

Paxton, A. and Dale, R. (2017). Interpersonal movement synchrony responds to high- and low-level conversational constraints. *Frontiers in Psychology*, 8.

Pentland, A. S. (2008). *Honest Signals: How They Shape Our World*. The MIT Press.

Pickering, M. and Ferreira, V. (2008). Structural priming: A critical review. *Psychological Bulletin*, 134(3):427–459, May.

Pickering, M. and Garrod, S. (2004). Toward a mechanistic psychology of dialogue. *The Behavioral and brain sciences*, 27:169–90; discussion 190, 05.

Priego-Valverde, B., Bigi, B., Attardo, S., Pickering, L., and Gironzetti, E. (2018). Is smiling during humor so obvious? A cross-cultural comparison of smiling behavior in humorous sequences in American English and French interactions. *Intercultural Pragmatics*.

Priego-Valverde, B., Bigi, B., and Amoyal, M. (2020). "Cheese!": A corpus of face-to-face French interactions. A case study for analyzing smiling and conversational humor. In *Language Resources and Evaluation Conference*, pages 460–468, Marseille, France.

Rauzy, S. and Amoyal, M. (2020). SMAD: A tool for automatically annotating the smile intensity along a video record. In *HRC2020, 10th Humour Research Conference*.

Schmidt, R. C. P., Morr, S., Fitzpatrick, P., and Richardson, M. J. (2012). Measuring the dynamics of interactional synchrony. *Journal of Nonverbal Behavior*, 36(4):263–279.

Seibt, B., Mühlberger, A., Likowski, K., and Weyers, P. (2015). Facial mimicry in its social setting. *Frontiers in Psychology*, 6.

Proceedings of the Smiling and Laughter across Contexts and the Life-span Workshop @LREC2022, pages 21–25
Marseille, 24 June 2022

Analysis of Co-Laughter Gesture Relationship on RGB videos in Dyadic Conversation Context

Hugo Bohy$_1$, Ahmad Hammoudeh$_{123}$, Antoine Maiorca$_1$, Stéphane Dupont$_2$, Thierry Dutoit$_{13}$
[1] ISIA Lab, [2] MAIA Lab,[3] TRAIL
[1,2] University of Mons, Mons, Belgium, [3] Wallonia-Brussels Federation, Belgium
{hugo.bohy, 535653, antoine.maiorca, stephane.dupont, thierry.dutoit}@umons.ac.be

Abstract

The development of virtual agents has enabled human-avatar interactions to become increasingly rich and varied. Moreover, an expressive virtual agent i.e. that mimics the natural expression of emotions, enhances social interaction between a user (human) and an agent (intelligent machine). The set of non-verbal behaviors of a virtual character is, therefore, an important component in the context of human-machine interaction. Laughter is not just an audio signal, but an intrinsic relationship of multimodal non-verbal communication, in addition to audio, it includes facial expressions and body movements. Motion analysis often relies on a relevant motion capture dataset, but the main issue is that the acquisition of such a dataset is expensive and time-consuming. This work studies the relationship between laughter and body movements in dyadic conversations. The body movements were extracted from videos using deep learning based pose estimator model. We found that, in the explored *NDC-ME* dataset, a single statistical feature (i.e, the maximum value, or the maximum of Fourier transform) of a joint movement weakly correlates with laughter intensity by 30%. However, we did not find a direct correlation between audio features and body movements. We discuss about the challenges to use such dataset for the audio-driven co-laughter motion synthesis task.

Keywords: Co-Laughter Motion Analysis, Natural Dyadic Conversation

1. Introduction

The interactive gesture generation task aims to control the gesture of a virtual character with a user control signal. Many works addressed the problem of synthesizing the gesture of an avatar along with a speech modality (Alexanderson et al., 2020; Ahuja et al., 2020). These methods enabled capturing and synthesis of natural co-speech gestures of a virtual character. (Kucherenko et al., 2020) used speech and text jointly as inputs to their proposed model to generate the gestures and reported that the multimodal aspect of their method helps to understand the sentence semantics and outputs natural and diverse gestures. (Yoon et al., 2020) encoded these modalities along with the speaker identity since each expressive behavior highly relies on the speaker.

Nevertheless, motion synthesis from a non-verbal audio input such as laughter is a complex task where no a priori semantic information is available with the audio signal to help with understanding the overall context. However, laughter constitutes an important part of social interaction (McKeown and Curran, 2015) where the smiling and laughing expression of an interlocutor induces a mimicry effect on each partner (El Haddad et al., 2019). The growing interest in virtual environments has led to the development of virtual social agents. The immersive factor of a virtual world is partly induced by the naturalness of the motion of virtual characters. The human-avatar social interaction is an active research topic among the computer vision community and rendering natural motion is a crucial task to enhance the social aspect of the avatar (Garau, 2003). Co-laughter gesture synthesis is thus a relevant task in human computer interaction where it can be exploited in various use cases such as video game development (Mancini et al., 2013) or in a medical context e.g. to enhance the social skills of children with autism spectrum disorder (Didehbani et al., 2016).

The work presented in this paper falls in a wider project aiming at generating co-laughter motion corresponding to the audio given at its input using generative deep neural networks. We present here first analyses results on the relationship between body movements (excluding facial expressions) and several aspects of laughter. These analyses would help us gain a better understanding of our data and thus organize their use to build the previously mentioned generative system. The motion data is not extracted from motion capture sensors but is estimated from the recorded RGB videos directly. Neural networks are powerful tools for learning complex relationships between given modalities within a database. Thus, the proposed analysis allows us to identify whether correlations between laughter, its intensity and the associated movement are significant within a given dataset. If this dataset does not exhibit a high correlation between laughter and body motion, it may be a challenging dataset to train neural networks that synthesize body motion from audio laughter.

This paper is organized as follow: Section 2 reviews the state-of-the-art analysis of the relationship between multiple laughter modalities and co-laughter motion synthesis methods. Section 3 explains the experimental protocol and Section 4 analyzes the experimental results. Section 5 discusses the limitations of this work and proposes some improvements.

2. Related Work

To focus on the synthesis task, it is useful to understand and measure the relationship between laughter as an audio signal and the gesture performed during that laughter. (Griffin et al., 2013) found a significant contrast in the captured motions between different types of laughter (hilarious, social, and non-laughter) and claimed that motion features analysis helped with the classification of laughter type. (Niewiadomski et al., 2016) showed that full-body motion features are sufficient to detect laughter occurrences. (Mancini et al., 2013) pointed out the periodic pattern of the shoulder motion while laughing in the dataset *Multimodal Multiperson Corpus of Laughter in Interaction* (Niewiadomski et al., 2013). (Ishi et al., 2019) focused on laughter intensity to reveal that the degree of smiling face and the occurrences of the front, back, up, and down motions are proportional to the laughter intensity.

(DiLorenzo et al., 2008) proposes a physics-based model to synthesize the torso deformation induces by the air flow while laughing. (Niewiadomski et al., 2014) performs a harmonic analysis of the laughter body motions to get relevant rhythmic features for the generation of body movements. (Ding et al., 2017) synthesized upper body gestures from laughter audio signal based on the captured or defined co-laughter motion correlations. Their approach is based on a statistical framework for head and torso motion and a rule-based method for shoulder motion due to the limitation of their dataset. (Ishi et al., 2019) generated co-speech and laughter motion (eyelids, face, hand and upper body) on physical android robots. The works presented above relied on recorded motion capture datasets of people laughing in multiple contexts. (Jokinen et al., 2016) analyzed videos of social interactions and pointed out the synchrony of body movements with laughter. Similarly, this research aims to identify body motion relationships with laughter from RGB videos and audio signals. However, (Jokinen et al., 2016) estimated bounding boxes around the limbs of the participants.

This work proposes an analysis of the relationship between low-level motion features extracted from RGB videos i.e. the Cartesian position of each joint, the laughter intensity and audio features in the context of a dyadic conversation. This relational study aims to identify any significant correlation between the positions of the joints and the laughter audio signal and intensity. Two approaches are tested and are further explained in Section 3.2.1 regarding the laughter audio signal: first, the audio signal is decomposed into a set of low-level and physical features and then the audio signals are embedded into a latent space from the baseline speech oriented model *Wav2vec 2.0* (Baevski et al., 2020). Finally, the relationship between the 2D Cartesian positions of the skeleton and laughter intensity is established and described in Section 3.2.2.

3. Experiments

3.1. Dataset

In our experiments, we used the dataset *Naturalistic Dyadic Conversation on Moral Emotions* (*NDC-ME*) (Heron et al., 2018). It consists of a collection of dyadic conversations focusing on moral emotions through speaker-listener interactions. In contrast to *IFADV* Corpus (van Son et al., 2008) and the *Cardiff Conversation Database* (Aubrey et al., 2013), the whole upper body of the participants is available in the videos and their motion is not constrained by any object. 21 pairs of participants have been recorded while they were interacting together without following a fixed scenario. The audio and videos have been captured separately. The emotions and the intensity of the expressed emotion of each participant during the recording have been labeled using the annotation tool *ELAN* (Max Planck Institute for Psycholinguistics, 2022) and are available here [1]. The annotation rules follow the protocol [2] used by (El Haddad et al., 2019). The laughter clips are also labeled into 3 categories regarding their intensity: low, medium, and high. At that time, only 7 pairs have been annotated. Following these annotations, the audio and videos in which laughter occurs are extracted from the initial dataset. 186 videos are kept including 10 male and 4 female speakers for a total duration of 199.33 seconds. Then, 2D Cartesian positions of the skeleton joints are extracted from the RGB videos using *OpenPose* (Cao et al., 2018). The skeleton consists of 8 joints representing the upper body of the subject. A frame sample with an estimated skeleton as well as the upper body structure is shown in Figure 1.

3.2. Experimental setup

This part describes the experimental protocol to identify the correlation between the laughter modalities in *NDC-ME* dataset.

Joint movement signals are represented as time series s where $s^i_j = p^i_j - \bar{p_j}$ with p^i_j, the Cartesian position of a joint j at frame i and $\bar{p_j}$ the mean position of the joint j. Thus, s_j is the temporal fluctuations of the position of the joint j around its mean position. Then, the horizontal and vertical component of the motion signal of joint j are respectively noted x_j and y_j. In this work, we consider separately horizontal and vertical movements for the sake of simplicity but it would be interesting to consider both directions. The correlations on

[1] https://zenodo.org/record/3820510

[2] This protocol is available here

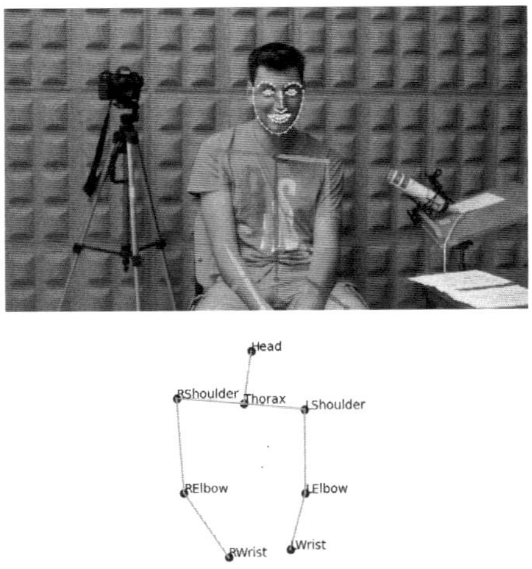

Figure 1: Top: sample of a video with the estimated skeleton and face landmarks. Since this work only focuses on the body skeleton, the face landmarks are ignored. Bottom: structure of the upper body skeleton.

shoulders, elbows and wrists are computed separately for the right and left body parts and we further report the average value.

3.2.1. Body movement and audio features

We wanted to analyse the correlation between the audio signal and the body movement. For the audio signal, we extracted two sets of features per 20 ms frame : one that includes 19 well-known low-level features in the speech analysis domain (3 from LPC, 13 MFCCs and 3 LPCCs), and the other that includes the 512 embedded outputs of the *Wav2vec 2.0* model. For each subset of features, we computed the pearson correlation coefficient between (x_j, y_j) and the time series of audio features.

3.2.2. Body movements and laughter intensity

Firstly, the following features were extracted for each horizontal and vertical joint movement signal (x_j, y_j): In the time domain (power P, maximum amplitude value max, mean value μ and standard deviation σ), and the frequency domain (the maximum value of Fourier Transform $max(FT)$, the mean of Fourier Transform $\mu(FT)$, and peak frequency $f_{pk} = argmax(FT)$). Since laughter videos vary in length, Fourier Transform curves were linearly interpolated in 248 uniform samples between 0 and Nyquist frequency $f_{Nyquist}$. The upper 10% of the frequency range was excluded when finding the peak frequency in order to exclude high-frequency noise ($f_{pk} < 0.9 f_{Nyquist}$). The correlation between those extracted features of joints movement and laughter intensity are then analyzed.

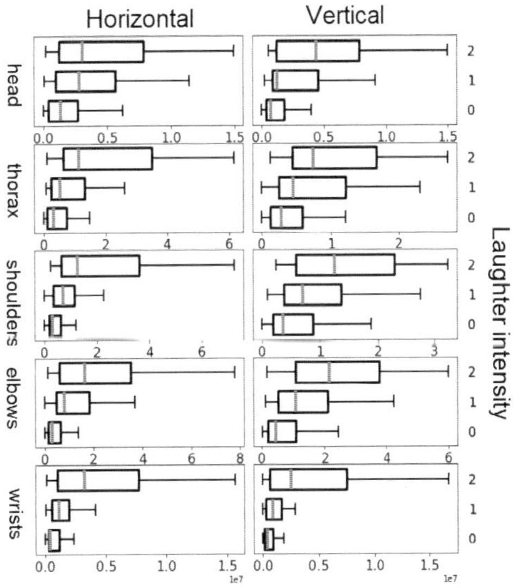

Figure 2: The maximum Fourier transform of a joint movement signal $max(FT(p_j))$ under multiple laughter intensities. Each Row represents a joint and each column represents a direction of movement (horizontal/vertical). Each figure has 3 boxplots (low laughter intensity at 0, medium at 1, and high at 2). The orange line in a boxplot represents the mean.

4. Results

Section 4 presents the results of the correlation analysis between body movements, audio features and laughter intensity.

4.1. Body movements and audio features

Table 1 shows the maximum average correlation between an audio feature and a joint movement. The values depicted informs us about the weak correlation between the evolution of the position of a joint compared to the evolution of an audio feature. However, using embedded features rather than interpretable ones increases the correlation across all joints.

4.2. Body movements and laughter intensity

The correlation between the extracted features and laughter intensity is shown in table 2. Since $max(FT)$ feature has the highest correlation, we visualized the distribution of $max(FT)$ features under multiple laughter intensities in Figure 2. The visualization of $max(FT)$, similar to the other extracted features, resulted in overlapping boxplots. Hence, we conclude that any of the extracted features alone is not sufficient to identify the laughter intensity. However, statistically speaking, the mean value of the distribution (the orange line in Figure 2) increases with laughter intensity.

Feature	Horizontal Movement					Vertical Movement				
	Head	**Thorax**	**Shoulders**	**Elbows**	**Wrists**	**Head**	**Thorax**	**Shoulders**	**Elbows**	**Wrists**
LPC	0.03	0.02	0.05	0.03	0.02	0.04	0.05	0.07	0.02	0.03
MFCCs	-0.03	-0.01	0.01	-0.01	0.01	-0.08	-0.06	-0.06	-0.04	-0.01
LPCCs	0.05	0.03	0.04	-0.01	-0.01	0.05	0.07	0.07	-0.02	0.08
W2V	**0.09**	**0.08**	**0.07**	**0.08**	**0.09**	**0.11**	**0.09**	**0.09**	**0.10**	**0.09**

Table 1: Maximum average correlation between an audio feature and a joint with respect to its movement direction.

Feature	Horizontal Movement					Vertical Movement				
	Head	**Thorax**	**Shoulders**	**Elbows**	**Wrists**	**Head**	**Thorax**	**Shoulders**	**Elbows**	**Wrists**
max	0.09	0.25	0.30	0.22	0.26	0.26	**0.39**	**0.25**	0.25	0.20
P	0.08	0.09	0.18	0.10	0.13	0.29	0.25	0.16	0.10	0.10
μ	0.10	0.05	0.06	0.02	0.08	-0.17	-0.19	-0.14	-0.16	-0.15
σ	0.16	0.23	0.28	0.23	0.26	0.35	0.31	0.21	0.27	0.20
$\mu(FT)$	0.13	0.26	0.30	0.24	0.26	0.28	0.37	0.23	0.25	0.18
max(FT)	0.23	**0.32**	**0.36**	**0.32**	**0.34**	**0.36**	0.33	0.24	**0.32**	**0.21**
fpk	**-0.29**	-0.22	-0.20	-0.2	-0.22	-0.22	-0.21	-0.12	-0.20	-0.12

Table 2: Correlation between laughter intensity and a joint movement feature. The power P, maximum amplitude value max, mean value μ and standard deviation σ are computed from the horizontal and vertical motion signals in the time domain. In the frequency domain, the motion features are the maximum value of Fourier Transform $max(FT)$, the mean of Fourier Transform $\mu(FT)$ and and peak frequency f_{pk}. The correlation is bound between -1 and 1. The higher absolute value means a stronger correlation and 0 shows no correlation in the data.

5. Discussion and Challenges

The results presented in Section 4 indicate that, in *NDC-ME* dataset, body movements and audio features seem to be weakly correlated. Further investigation and processing are needed to draw a more robust conclusions. Thus, this dataset seems, at the moment and with this current analysis, challenging for a co-laughter gesture synthesis task. However, we found some aspects in the dataset that might impact the results in our analysis: in some files, speaker speech overlaps with the listener's laughter and we suspect that this influenced the experimental results in Section 4. These need to be removed from the dataset in future work to get more accurate results. One suggestion is the application of channel source separation methods to the audio to distinguish the laughter or speech of each participant and have a better audio representation (more suitable features). Then, the laughter intensity has been subjectively annotated by a single annotator and having a low number of annotators makes the data distribution more sensitive to human error. We suggest to increase the number of annotators and e.g. extracting the mean annotations to reduce this impact. Moreover, since the dataset has not been fully annotated yet, it contains a relatively small amount of laughter examples. Then, in a future work, we would like to extract correlations from audio acoustic features such as pitch or loudness. Moreover, it would be interesting to take into account other modalities such as the type of laughter and the context of the interactions. Finally, in this work, we focus on body movement but face landmarks are available from the *OpenPose* estimation as shown in Figure 1. The relationship between those landmarks and the laughter intensity and laughter audio features can be established in further investigation.

6. Conclusion

This work proposes a method to analyze the relationship between laughter, its intensity and the body movement in recorded dyadic conversations. In contrast with previous works, the gestures are extracted from the RGB videos using a baseline pose estimation method. First, this work highlights around 30% correlation between laughter intensity and motion features where the maximum amplitude of the Fourier transform leads to the highest correlation value. Moreover, the analysis of correlation between interpretable and high-level audio features does not output significant correlation values. This work highlights some of the limitations of *NDC-ME* dataset that we need to take into account in the context of deep generative model training for body motion generation from a laughter audio signal. This analysis opens the way to create datasets suited to build multimodal models that generate the motion of virtual agents from the audio cue.

7. Acknowledgements

This work was supported by Service Public de Wallonie Recherche under grant n° 2010235 - *ARIAC* by *DIGITALWALLONIA4.AI*

8. Bibliographical References

Ahuja, C., Lee, D. W., Ishii, R., and Morency, L.-P. (2020). No gestures left behind: Learning relationships between spoken language and freeform gestures. In *Findings of the Association for Computational Linguistics: EMNLP 2020*, pages 1884–1895, Online, November. Association for Computational Linguistics.

Alexanderson, S., Henter, G. E., Kucherenko, T., and Beskow, J. (2020). Style-controllable speech-driven gesture synthesis using normalising flows. *Computer Graphics Forum*, 39(2):487–496.

Aubrey, A. J., Marshall, D., Rosin, P. L., Vendeventer, J., Cunningham, D. W., and Wallraven, C. (2013). Cardiff conversation database (ccdb): A database of natural dyadic conversations. In *Proceedings of the IEEE Conference on Computer Vision and Pattern Recognition Workshops*, pages 277–282.

Baevski, A., Zhou, H., Mohamed, A., and Auli, M. (2020). wav2vec 2.0: A framework for self-supervised learning of speech representations. *CoRR*, abs/2006.11477.

Cao, Z., Hidalgo, G., Simon, T., Wei, S., and Sheikh, Y. (2018). Openpose: Realtime multi-person 2d pose estimation using part affinity fields. *CoRR*, abs/1812.08008.

Didehbani, N., Allen, T., Kandalaft, M., Krawczyk, D., and Chapman, S. (2016). Virtual reality social cognition training for children with high functioning autism. *Computers in human behavior*, 62:703–711.

DiLorenzo, P. C., Zordan, V. B., and Sanders, B. L. (2008). Laughing out loud: Control for modeling anatomically inspired laughter using audio. In *ACM SIGGRAPH Asia 2008 papers*, pages 1–8.

Ding, Y., Huang, J., and Pelachaud, C. (2017). Audio-driven laughter behavior controller. *IEEE Transactions on Affective Computing*, 8(4):546–558.

El Haddad, K., Chakravarthula, S. N., and Kennedy, J. (2019). Smile and laugh dynamics in naturalistic dyadic interactions: Intensity levels, sequences and roles. In *2019 International Conference on Multimodal Interaction*, pages 259–263.

Garau, M. (2003). *The impact of avatar fidelity on social interaction in virtual environments*. University of London, University College London (United Kingdom).

Griffin, H. J., Aung, M. S., Romera-Paredes, B., McLoughlin, C., McKeown, G., Curran, W., and Bianchi-Berthouze, N. (2013). Laughter type recognition from whole body motion. In *2013 Humaine Association Conference on Affective Computing and Intelligent Interaction*, pages 349–355.

Heron, L., Kim, J., Lee, M., El Haddad, K., Dupont, S., Dutoit, T., and Truong, K. (2018). A dyadic conversation dataset on moral emotions. In *2018 13th IEEE International Conference on Automatic Face & Gesture Recognition (FG 2018)*, pages 687–691. IEEE.

Ishi, C. T., Minato, T., and Ishiguro, H. (2019). Analysis and generation of laughter motions, and evaluation in an android robot. *APSIPA Transactions on Signal and Information Processing*, 8.

Jokinen, K., Trong, T. N., and Wilcock, G. (2016). Body movements and laughter recognition: experiments in first encounter dialogues. In *Proceedings of the Workshop on Multimodal Analyses enabling Artificial Agents in Human-Machine Interaction*, pages 20–24.

Kucherenko, T., Jonell, P., van Waveren, S., Henter, G. E., Alexanderson, S., Leite, I., and Kjellström, H. (2020). Gesticulator: A framework for semantically-aware speech-driven gesture generation. In *Proceedings of the ACM International Conference on Multimodal Interaction*.

Mancini, M., Ach, L., Bantegnie, E., Baur, T., Berthouze, N., Datta, D., Ding, Y., Dupont, S., Griffin, H. J., Lingenfelser, F., et al. (2013). Laugh when you're winning. In *International Summer Workshop on Multimodal Interfaces*, pages 50–79. Springer.

Max Planck Institute for Psycholinguistics, T. L. A. (2022). Elan (version 6.3) [computer software]. Retrieved from `https://archive.mpi.nl/tla/elan`.

McKeown, G. and Curran, W. (2015). The relationship between laughter intensity and perceived humour. In *The 4th Interdisciplinary Workshop on Laughter and other Non-Verbal Vocalisations in Speech, Enschede, Netherlands*, pages 27–29.

Niewiadomski, R., Mancini, M., Baur, T., Varni, G., Griffin, H., and Aung, M. S. H. (2013). Mmli: Multimodal multiperson corpus of laughter in interaction. In Albert Ali Salah, et al., editors, *Human Behavior Understanding*, pages 184–195, Cham. Springer International Publishing.

Niewiadomski, R., Mancini, M., Ding, Y., Pelachaud, C., and Volpe, G. (2014). Rhythmic body movements of laughter. In *Proceedings of the 16th international conference on multimodal interaction*, pages 299–306.

Niewiadomski, R., Mancini, M., Varni, G., Volpe, G., and Camurri, A. (2016). Automated laughter detection from full-body movements. *IEEE Transactions on Human-Machine Systems*, 46(1):113–123.

van Son, R., Wesseling, W., Sanders, E., and van den Heuvel, H. (2008). The ifadv corpus: A free dialog video corpus. In *Proceedings of the Sixth International Conference on Language Resources and Evaluation (LREC'08)*.

Yoon, Y., Cha, B., Lee, J.-H., Jang, M., Lee, J., Kim, J., and Lee, G. (2020). Speech gesture generation from the trimodal context of text, audio, and speaker identity. *ACM Transactions on Graphics*, 39(6).

Proceedings of the Smiling and Laughter across Contexts and the Life-span Workshop @LREC2022, page 26
Marseille, 24 June 2022

You Make Me Laugh! Friends, Strangers and Neurodiversity

Ceci Qing Cai1, Lucie Vigreux1, Manying Chiu1, Bangjie Wang1, Alexis Macintyre1, Sarah White1, and Sophie Scott1

Institute of Cognitive Neuroscience, University College London
Alexandra House, 17-19 Queen Square, London WC1N 3AZ
q.cai.17@ucl.ac.uk, man.chiu.19@alumni.ucl.ac.uk, bangjie.wang.18@ucl.ac.uk, l.vigreux@ucl.ac.uk, s.white@ucl.ac.uk, sophie.scott@ucl.ac.uk

Abstract

Laughter is a positive emotional expression, however, its presence and usage as communicative tool is understudied in autism research. Limited research has focused on autistic children and found that they used laughter for expressing happiness and mirth, but rarely used it for social purposes compared to their neurotypical (NT) peers. To date, no research has included autistic adults.

The current study aims to investigate 1) the difference in laughter behaviour between pairs of one autistic and one neurotypical adult (MIXED dyads) and age-, gender- and IQ-matched pairs of two neurotypical adults (NT dyads); 2) whether the closeness of relationship (Friends/Strangers) would influence laughter production.

In total, 30 MIXED and 29 NT dyads in the Stranger condition and 7 MIXED dyads and 12 NT dyads in the Friend condition were engaged in a conversational task and a video-watching task and their laughter was extracted, quantified and annotated. We calculated the Total duration of laughter and Shared laughter in each dyad.

Regardless of the closeness of relationship, MIXED dyads produced significantly less Total laughter than NT dyads in both tasks. The same tendency was also found for Shared laughter, although participants shared more laughter during video-watching than conversation and this tendency was more pronounced for NT than MIXED dyads. Strikingly, NT dyads produced more shared laughter when interacting with their friend than with a stranger during video-watching task, whilst the amount of shared laughter in MIXED dyads did not differ when interacting with their friend or a stranger.

These findings may indicate that autistic adults show a different pattern of laughter production relative to NT adults during social communication. However, it is also possible that a mismatch between autistic and NT communication, and specifically in existing friendships, may have resulted in patterns of laughter more akin to that seen between strangers.

Keywords: laughter, nonverbal behaviour, dyadic study, autism, social communication, relationship

Proceedings of the Smiling and Laughter across Contexts and the Life-span Workshop @LREC2022, page 27
Marseille, 24 June 2022

Intergroup Bias in Smile Discrimination in Autism

Ruihan Wu, Antonia Hamilton, Sarah White
Institute of Cognitive Neuroscience, University College London
Alexandra House, 17-19 Queen Square, London WC1N 3AZ
{r.wu.16, a.hamilton, s.white}@ucl.ac.uk

Abstract

Genuine and posed smiles are important social cues (Song, Over, & Carpenter, 2016). Autistic individuals struggle to reliably differentiate between them (Blampied, Johnston, Miles, & Liberty, 2010; Boraston, Corden, Miles, Skuse, & Blakemore, 2008), which may contribute to their difficulties in understanding others' mental states. An intergroup bias has been found in non-autistic adults in identifying genuine from posed smiles (Young, 2017). This is the first study designed to investigate if autistic individuals would show a different pattern when differentiating smiles for in-groups and out-groups. Fifty-nine autistic adults were compared with forty non-autistic adults, matched on sex, age and nonverbal IQ. Roughly, half of each group were further randomly separated into two groups with a minimal group paradigm (adapted from Howard & Rothbart, 1980). There was no real difference between the groups, participants were primed to believe they were more similar to their in-groups. The ability to distinguish smiles was assessed on a 7-point Likert scale. We found both autism and non-autism groups rated genuine smiles more genuine than posed smiles and in-groups more genuine than out-groups. Even though both groups identified themselves more as in-group than out-group members, autistic individuals were less likely to than non-autistic individuals. However, autistic participants generally rated smiles as less genuine than non-autistic counterparts. These results indicate that autistic adults are capable of identifying genuine smiles from posed smiles, unlike previous findings; but they may be less convinced of the genuineness of others, which may affect their social communication thereafter. Importantly, autistic adults were equally influenced by social intergroup biases which has the potential to be used in interventions to alleviate their social difficulties in daily lives.

Keywords: smile, autism, intergroup bias

References

Blampied, M., Johnston, L., Miles, L., & Liberty, K. (2010). Sensitivity to differences between enjoyment and non-enjoyment smiles in children with autism spectrum disorder. British journal of developmental psychology, 28(2), 483-489.

Boraston, Z. L., Corden, B., Miles, L. K., Skuse, D. H., & Blakemore, S.-J. (2008). Brief report: Perception of genuine and posed smiles by individuals with autism. Journal of autism and developmental disorders, 38(3), 574-580.

Howard, J. W., & Rothbart, M. (1980). Social categorization and memory for in-group and out-group behavior. Journal of personality and social psychology, 38(2), 301.

Song, R., Over, H., & Carpenter, M. (2016). Young children discriminate genuine from fake smiles and expect people displaying genuine smiles to be more prosocial. Evolution and Human Behavior, 37(6), 490-501.

Young, S. G. (2017). An outgroup advantage in discriminating between genuine and posed smiles. Self and Identity, 16(3), 298-312.

Proceedings of the Smiling and Laughter across Contexts and the Life-span Workshop @LREC2022, pages 28–29
Marseille, 24 June 2022

Inhalation Noises as Endings of Laughs in Conversational Speech

Jürgen Trouvain[1], Raphael Werner[1], Khiet P. Truong[2]
[1]Saarland University, [2]University of Twente
[1]Dept. Language Science and Technology, Geb. C7.2, D-66123 Saarbrücken
[2]Human Media Interaction, P.O. Box 217, NL-7500 AE Enschede
{trouvain, rwerner}@lst.uni-saarland.de, k.p.truong@utwente.nl

Abstract

In this study we investigate the role of inhalation noises at the end of laughter events in two conversational corpora that provide relevant annotations. A re-annotation of the categories for laughter, silence and inbreath noises enabled us to see that inhalation noises terminate laughter events in the majority of all inspected laughs with a duration comparable to inbreath noises initiating speech phases. This type of corpus analysis helps to understand the mechanisms of audible respiratory activities in speaking vs. laughing in conversations.

Keywords: inhalation, laughter, respiratory control

1. Introduction

In this study we investigate the role of inhalation noises in laughter events in corpus data of conversational speech. The (German) GRASS corpus (Schuppler et al., 2014) provides annotations on laughter and inbreath noises which were helpful for the further analysis of audible respiratory activities in speaking vs. laughing in conversations. It is hypothesised that inhalation noises mark the end of many laughs whereas in speech production, inhalation noises usually mark the beginning of speech sections. The aims of this preliminary investigation are threefold: 1) to learn more about control mechanisms of audible inhalation, 2) to refine our knowledge of the composition of complex laughs, and 3) to develop routines for re-annotations of laughter events in corpora.

Laugh events can show a great range of diversity and variability or as (Bachorowski and Owren, 2001) put it: "Not all laughs are alike". This is also reflected in various degrees of complexity (Truong et al., 2019). Noises of inhalation (or inbreath) but also silent phases can be important constituents of laughs.

During tidal breathing, i.e. when not speaking, inhalation is usually not acoustically audible. However, while talking, inhalation is often (but not necessarily) reflected as noise. Inhalation noises usually occur shortly before a speech section starts or in pauses of larger speech sections, but very infrequently after speech sections (Werner et al., 2021). In contrast, informal observations of complex laughs show that those laughs are often accompanied by a terminating inhalation noise (Truong et al., 2019) with a stretch of silence between the voiced phase and the inhalation phase, as illustrated in Fig. 1. It should be borne in mind that full-fledged isolated "laughter consistently lead to sudden and substantial decrease in lung volume" and that returning to regular tidal breathing needed two to three breath cycles after the laugh (Filippelli et al., 2001).

Silences preceding inbreath noises were analysed as part of the entire laugh event (Truong et al., 2019), i.e that silence does not mean that the laugh is over. However, in conversational corpora often silences and inbreath noises are marked as own categories that are not belonging to the laugh (Truong and Trouvain, 2012). Although labelled as "silence", it should not be regarded as strict silence in an acoustic-phonetic sense since there are sometimes nearly unnoticeable acoustic events which might be reflections of nearly quiet chuckling.

In general we can assume that in conversations, speakers obviously have different patterns of control on the inhalation for speaking, laughing and being quiet. It is thus the question how often laughs are terminated with inhalation noises and to determine the temporal shapes of those inhalation noises and their preceding silences.

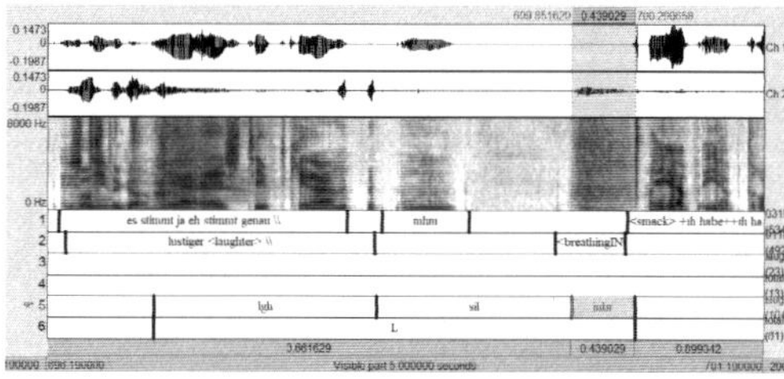

Figure 1: Example of a laugh from the GRASS corpus (Schuppler et al., 2014), speaker 2, dialogue 3, 696-700 sec. The intervals for "laughter" and "breathing IN" were copied from the original annotation (tier 2) to the laugh elements on tier 5, now with the core element ("lgh"), the silence ("sil") and the inbreath noise ("inbr"). All elements form the entire laugh ("L" on tier 6). The interval for "inbr" (in colour) was slightly corrected.

2. Methods

For this purpose, we investigated a subset of the main part of the GRASS corpus (Schuppler et al., 2014) containing conversational speech in German (between friends or relatives). From there the beginning sections of 900 sec of 3 dyadic conversations were taken. Laughter and inbreath noise were annotated with extra labels, many times within larger intervals. Often, the inbreath noise was not in the same annotation interval as the laugh, and possible silent phases preceding an inbreath noise and the final inbreath noise were not regarded as parts of the laugh. Thus, a separate annotation and a re-annotation for the laugh including the breath noise was needed (cp. also (Truong and Trouvain, 2012).

Single elements of a laugh were either the core element of a laugh (copied from the original annotation), speech-laughs, silent phase, and inbreath noise. Laughs were then categorised as either with a final inbreath noise or not. There were also sequences of laugh-inhalation-speech where the inbreath noise could be theoretically regarded as part of the laugh or of speech or as we did of both. Those cases occurred in about 10% of all cases with an inbreath noise.

3. Results and discussion

Counting the frequency of laughs shows that laughs with terminating inbreath noises are in the majority (two out of three) compared to those laughs that do not contain a final inbreath noise. Silent phases occurred in about three quarters of all cases before a final inbreath noise in those laughs. All inspected individual speakers showed terminating inbreath noise when laughing. However, for some individuals this type of laughter was not dominant.

Looking at the duration of the entire laugh events reveals that laughs with terminating inbreath noises are generally longer than those without inbreath noises. One the one hand this can be easily explained by the fact that inbreath noise and the potential preceding silence considerably contribute to the total duration of individual laughs. On the other hand, longer laughs can have a natural tendency to more intense air consumption which requires a deeper and therefore audible inhalation. There is also a tendency that the 'core' element in laughs with an inbreath noise ending is longer than in laughs without an inbreath noise.

Concentrating on the duration of the inbreath noises we can see rather constant average values for individual speakers: from 250 ms up to 480 ms with standard deviations of around 100 ms. These numbers are in line with average values for inbreath noises for speech (Werner et al., 2021): in utterance-initial position, i.e. after a longer silence where speakers switch from tidal to speech breathing, the inbreath noises took 535 ms on average, in contrast to pauses within speech sections with a mean duration of 408 ms.

As a side observation we can report that the intensity in inbreath noises at the end of laughs is rather high compared to inbreath noises preceding speech. We assume that the air leakage during laughter requires deep inhalation which is not only reflected in shorter inhalation but also in a more salient acoustic shape.

4. Conclusions

Inbreath noises usually represent challenges when annotating laughs in corpora of conversational speech. Laughs with inbreath noises often need a re-annotation (Truong and Trouvain, 2012)(Truong et al., 2019), as it was done here for one corpus. For such a procedure it is of great help to have a first annotation.

This study reveals that inbreath noises as final element of laughs seem to be an important component immanent to many and probably most laughs. Very often a silent period links the "core" of the laugh with the final inbreath noise.

In contrast to speaking, where inbreath noises usually occur at the beginning of a vocalisation section, in laughing they mark their end. Our explanation so far is that audible inhalation for speech is mainly a consequence of the planning of upcoming information whereas audible inhalation in laughter is a consequence of unplanned air leakage due to spontaneous vocalisation.

5. Bibliographical References

Bachorowski, J. A. and Owren, M. J. (2001). Not all laughs are alike: Voiced but not unvoiced laughter readily elicits positive affect. *Psychological Science*, 12:252 – 257.

Filippelli, M., Pellegrino, R., Iandelli, I., Misuri, G., Rodarte, J. R., Duranti, R., Brusasco, V., and Scano, G. (2001). Respiratory dynamics during laughter. *Journal of Applied Physiology*, 90(4):1441–1446.

Truong, K. P. and Trouvain, J. (2012). Laughter annotations in conversational speech corpora – possibilities and limitations for phonetic analysis. *Proc. 4th Workshop on Corpora for Research on Emotion Sentiment and Social Signals*, pages 20–24.

Truong, K. P., Trouvain, J., and Jansen, M.-P. (2019). Towards an Annotation Scheme for Complex Laughter in Speech Corpora. In *Proc. Interspeech 2019*, pages 529–533.

Werner, R., Fuchs, S., Trouvain, J., and Möbius, B. (2021). Inhalations in Speech: Acoustic and Physiological Characteristics. In *Proc. Interspeech 2021*, pages 3186–3190.

6. Language Resource References

Schuppler, B., Hagmueller, M., Morales-Cordovilla, J. A., and Pessentheiner, H. (2014). GRASS: the Graz corpus of read and spontaneous speech. In *Proc. 9th Language Resources and Evaluation Conference*, pages 1465–1470, Reykjavik, Iceland. ELRA.

Proceedings of the Smiling and Laughter across Contexts and the Life-span Workshop @LREC2022, pages 30–31
Marseille, 24 June 2022

Are there any Body-movement Differences between Women and Men when they Laugh?

Ahmad Hammoudeh[123], Antoine Maiorca[1], Stephane Dupont[2], Thierry Dutoit[13]
[1] ISIA Lab, [2]MAIA Lab, [3]TRAIL
[12]University of Mons, [123]Belgium
at.hammoudeh@gmail.com

Abstract

Initial computer-based experiments indicated more intense movement of women's shoulders and men's elbows, but further investigations are still needed.

Keywords: Laughter Motion Analysis, gender-based differences, behavioral pschology, gesture

1. Introduction

Smiling differences between men and women were reported (LaFrance 2000; 2003; 2013). Women smile more than men, especially between the age of 18 and 23. However, the expressiveness of females is not more across all facial actions (McDuff et al., 2017).

There are also body movement differences between males and females (Davis and Weitz, 1981). Male body posture, for example, was more open in (Cashdan, 1998).

Most these differences have been attributed to power, environemental, social, or cultural aspects in (Jäncke, 2018), yet the interaction between the influences and hormones levels are not fully understood.

2. Computer Based Analysis

We analyzed body movements of males and females when they laugh. Body movements were extracted from 186 laughter videos using OpenPose (Cao et al., 2019), which is a pose estimation deep learning model. The videos were taken from NDC-ME dataset (Heron et al., 2018).

The movement of a body part m was represented as time series s_m: $[s_m^1, s_m^2, \dots, s_m^n, \dots s_m^N]$, where s_m^n is the displacement of m in video frame n. $s_m^n = p_m^n - p_m^{n-1}$, where p_m^n is the cartesian position of m in frame n.

We compared body movement signals using the Fourier Transform. The frequency-domain was chosen to detect any potential artifact that could bias body movements signals (i.e., high-frequency noise from OpenPose).

3. Results

Fourier transform of thorax and shoulders movements were on average higher for females while males had higher Fourier transform of Elbows movement (see Figure 2). The difference became clearer with higher laughter intensities, and it was not limited to a small frequency range but covered most of the spectrum.

The results could be affected by the small size of the studied sample: 14 participants (different cultures/countries), 186 videos (38% for females). Other influencing factors could include age and context. Since all videos were recorded for sitting people in free dyadic conversation.

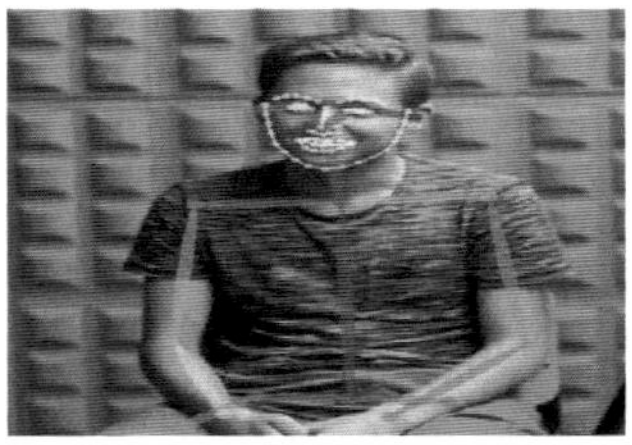

Figure 1 A sample pose extracted from a video.

4. Acknowledgements

This work was supported by Service Public de Wallonie Recherche under grant n° 2010235 ARIAC by DIGITALWALLONIA4.AI

5. Bibliographical References

Cashdan, E. (1998). Smiles, speech, and body posture: How women and men display sociometric status and power. Journal of Nonverbal Behavior, 22(4), 209-228

Cao, Z., Hidalgo, G., Simon, T., Wei, S., and Sheikh, Y. (2019). Openpose: Realtime multi-person 2d pose estimation using part affinity fields. In IEEE Transactions on Pattern Analysis and Machine Intelligence

Davis, M., & Weitz, S. (1981). Sex differences in body movements and positions. In Gender and nonverbal behavior (pp. 81-92). Springer, New York, NY

Heron, L., Kim, J., Lee, M., El Haddad, K., Dupont, S., Dutoit, T., and Truong, K. (2018). A dyadic conversation dataset on moral emotions. In 2018 13th IEEE International Conference on Automatic Face & Gesture Recognition (FG 2018), pages 687–691.

Jäncke, L. (2018). Sex/gender differences in cognition, neurophysiology, and neuroanatomy. F1000Research, 7.

LaFrance, M., & Hecht, M. A. (2000). Gender and smiling: A meta-analysis.

LaFrance, M., Hecht, M. A., & Paluck, E. L. (2003). The contingent smile: a meta-analysis of sex differences in smiling. Psychological bulletin, 129(2), 305.

LaFrance, M. (2013). Why smile?: The science behind facial expressions. WW Norton & Company.

McDuff, D., Kodra, E., Kaliouby, R. E., & LaFrance, M. (2017). A large-scale analysis of sex differences in facial expressions. PloS one, 12(4), e0173942.

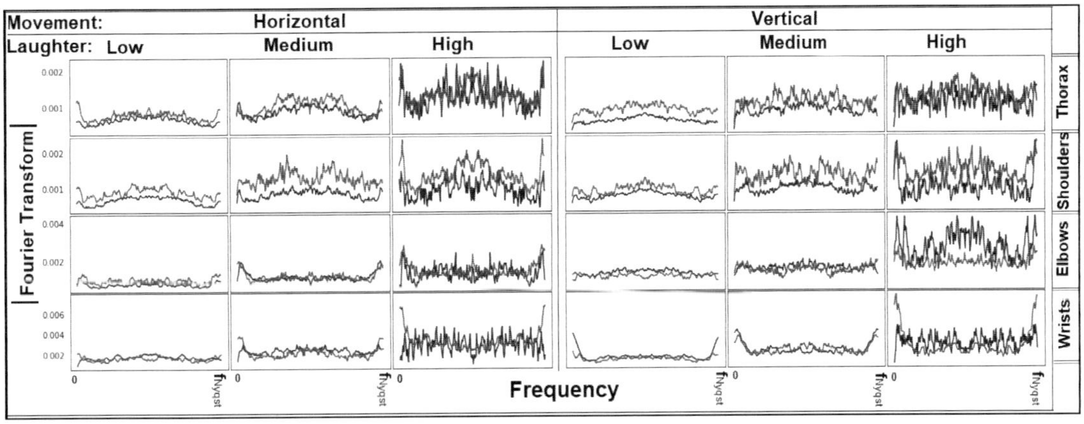

Figure 2 Average Fourier transform of a body part movement (red curves are for females, and the blue ones for males). Each Row represents a body part. Each column represents a pair of a laughter intensity (low/medium/high) and a direction of body part movement (horizontal/vertical). The x-axis represents the frequency between 0 and Nyquist frequency at 50 frames per second. The y-axis represents the mean amplitude of Fourier Transform.

Proceedings of the Smiling and Laughter across Contexts and the Life-span Workshop @LREC2022, pages 32–34
Marseille, 24 June 2022

Laughter in Cooperative and Competitive Settings

Magdalena Rychlowska, Gary McKeown, Ian Sneddon, William Curran
Queen's University Belfast
18-30 Malone Rd, Belfast BT9 5BN, United Kingdom
{m.rychlowska, g.mckeown, i.sneddon, w.curran}@qub.ac.uk

Abstract

This exploratory study investigates the extent to which social context influences the frequency of laughter. Fifty dyads of strangers played two simple laughter-inducing games. In a within-subjects design, we manipulated the setting in which the games were played. In the cooperative setting, the two participants worked together to earn money as a team and in the competitive setting, they competed against each other. We examined the frequency of laughs produced in cooperative and competitive settings. The analysis revealed a cross-over interaction between the setting and the type of the game that participants played. During a general knowledge quiz, participants tended to laugh more in the cooperative than in the competitive setting. However, the opposite was true when participants were asked to find a specific number of poker chips under time pressure. During this task participants laughed more in the competitive than in the cooperative setting. Together, the results highlight the flexibility of laughter as an interaction signal and illustrate the challenges of studying laughter in naturalistic settings.

Keywords: laughter, cooperation, competition, games

1. Introduction

Laughter is an extremely frequent social signal (Vettin and Todt, 2004), usually linked to amusement and humour (e.g., McKeown and Curran, 2015) but fulfills many other functions, ranging from turn-taking in conversation and speech coordination (Provine, 1993; Vettin and Todt, 2004) to signaling superiority and dominance (Kjeldgaard-Christiansen, 2018). The diversity of situations in which laughter is produced attests to its flexibility as an interaction signal.

Laughter also plays a pivotal role in promoting affiliation, developing cooperation, and regulating competitive behaviors (e.g., Bryant et al., 2016; Dunbar et al., 2021; Martin et al., 2017; Oveis et al., 2016). While laughter appears to be a key adaptive behavior facilitating social cohesion, little is understood about how laughter fulfills this function. We argue that laughter enhances social cohesion by virtue of its ambiguous nature, which allows its meaning to be determined by the social context in which it occurs.

The present study focuses on how social context influences laughter. Specifically, we compare laughter frequency in cooperative versus competitive contexts engineered to be as similar as possible, with the exception of inducing cooperation versus competition between participants. For this purpose, participants played two different laughter-inducing tasks: a general knowledge quiz and a game where participants had to find a specific number of poker chips under time pressure. Participants played both games twice: once in the cooperative setting, and once in the competitive setting. The study involved real-life monetary incentives, as subjects were led to believe that they would be paid depending on the outcome of each game. The analysis focused on examining the amount of laughter in the cooperative and the competitive context.

2. Method

2.1 Participants and Design

We recorded 50 dyads of participants (50 men, 50 women). Subjects were recruited from the general population via paper postings and were paid for their time.

The experiment followed a mixed design with the setting (cooperative vs. competitive) and type of task (general knowledge quiz vs. poker chip task) as within-subjects variables.

2.2 Stimuli

2.2.1 General Knowledge Quiz

Participants completed two general knowledge quizzes, one in the competitive setting, and the other in the cooperative setting. Each quiz involved 15 questions and was led by the experimenter playing the role of quizmaster. The experimenter read each question aloud and provided two response alternatives. Questions were selected to be challenging for participants, such that they were likely to hesitate before responding.

In the competitive quiz, participants were instructed to press a buzzer and submit their answers as quickly as possible. If their response was right, they received 1 point. If they were wrong, they received no points and the experimenter moved to the next question. The person who finished the quiz with more points won the round. Throughout the quiz, the experimenter attempted to keep participants' scores as close as possible, such that the outcome of the quiz remained uncertain until the end of the game. This was achieved by sometimes informing a respondent that their answer was wrong when, in fact, it was correct and vice versa. Questions were selected to be at a certain level of difficulty to enable this deception without detection.

In the cooperative quiz, participants worked together. After each question, they could discuss possible response options for up to 30 seconds before selecting the preferred response. They then pressed the buzzer and provided the final answer. If the answer was correct, the team received 1 point. In order to win the round, the team needed to finish the quiz with at least 10 points out of 15.

2.2.2 Poker Chip Task

Participants completed two versions of a task, in which they looked for poker chips in a large, opaque container filled with slime and containing 20 white chips, 10 red chips, and 10 blue chips. The container was closed and participants were asked to look for chips using the side

Figure 1: Participants during the poker chip task.

openings, such that the contents of the container remained invisible (see Figure 1). In the competitive setting, subjects were instructed to look for white chips. The person who found more chips within 2 minutes won the round. In the cooperative setting, participants worked as a team and had to find 10 red and 10 blue chips, also within 2 minutes. In both conditions, participants had to inform each other when they found any chips. They were also instructed to put every non-target chip (i.e., red or blue in the competitive condition, white in the cooperative condition) back in the box.

2.3 Procedure

Each session involved two same-gender individuals who did not know each other prior to the study. Upon arrival, participants provided informed consent and watched a 10-min video of silent comedy gags. Subjects were not recorded during this time and explicitly allowed to talk to each other. After watching the video, participants moved to the study area and sat facing each other at the table. Their faces and upper bodies were filmed with two webcams (Logitech HD Pro Webcam C920) and two microphones (HV577L Pro Headworn) connected to a MOTU 4Pre Audio interface recorded high-quality sound.

Participants played the two games in both competitive and cooperative contexts. The order of these settings was counterbalanced across dyads. Thus, each session involved playing four games. Participants were instructed that, depending on their performance, each of them could earn up to £2.50 for each game. Ostensibly, each person could be paid up to £10 for the entire study session. This reward was represented by stacks of poker chips that the experimenter increased or decreased depending on the outcome of each round. For games played in the competitive setting, only one participant could win the round and earn £2.50. For games played in the cooperative setting, both participants could win the round as a team and earn £2.50 each. The general knowledge quiz was always the first game that participants played, and was followed by the poker chip task, presented in the same (cooperative or competitive) setting. After that, a short break followed and participants watched another silent comedy video for 5 minutes. They then moved back to the studio room and were recorded during the second quiz and the poker chip task. Following each task, participants completed a short scale reporting how competitive they felt towards their partner and how much they thought they worked together. At the end of the study subjects were debriefed and every participant was paid £10 for their time.

2.4 Measures and Analytic Strategy

Recordings were annotated by four observers, two of them certified FACS coders. Observers annotated laughs for each of the four games. The annotations served to compute an indicator of laughs per minute, which was analyzed as a function of setting (cooperative vs. competitive) and task (general knowledge quiz vs. poker chip task). Given that the distribution of laughs per minute was strongly positively skewed, we transformed this measure using a cube root transformation.

3. Results

An examination of participants' perceptions of the extent to which they felt they worked together with their partner and how much they felt competitive towards this other person revealed a pattern of responses supporting the validity of our cooperative and competitive settings.

We used a linear mixed model with a by-participant random intercept (Barr et al., 2013; Bates et al., 2015; Magezi, 2015) to regress the cube root-transformed number of laughs per minute on setting (cooperative vs. competitive), task (general knowledge quiz vs. poker chip task), and their interaction.

Although the main effects of setting and task were significant, $B = 0.08$, $t(282.34) = 2.70$, $p = .01$ and $B = 0.10$, $t(281.62) = 3.29$, $p = .001$, respectively, they were qualified by a significant interaction, $B = -0.19$, $t(281.78) = -4.28$, $p < .001$, see Figure 2.

We therefore examined the effects of cooperative vs. competitive setting separately for the general knowledge quiz and for the poker chips task. This analysis revealed significant simple effects. Specifically, for the general knowledge quiz, the number of laughs per minute was higher in the cooperative ($M = 1.59$, $SD = 1.14$, non-transformed) than in the competitive condition ($M = 1.26$, $SD = 1.04$), $t(282) = 2.70$, $p = .01$. The opposite was true for the poker chip task – here, participants laughed more in the competitive ($M = 1.68$, $SD = 1.47$) than in the cooperative setting ($M = 1.25$, $SD = 1.06$), $t(283) = 3.34$, $p = .001$.

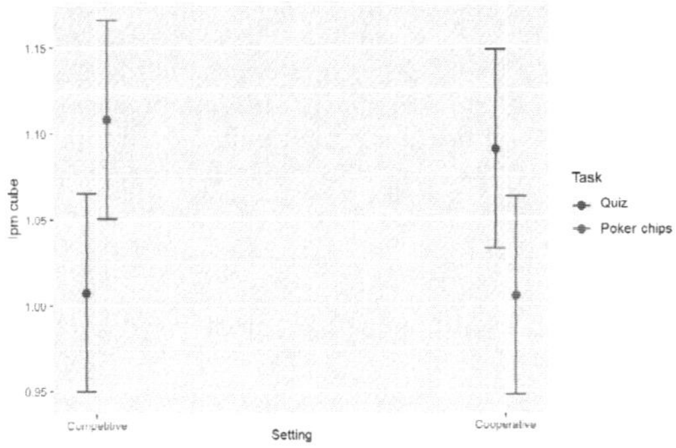

Figure 2: Effects of setting and task on number of laughs per minute

4. Discussion

In the current study, we predicted that participants would laugh more frequently in a cooperative setting than in a competitive setting. The analyses did not support this hypothesis. Instead of a general influence of cooperative versus competitive contexts, our findings suggest that the frequency of laughter is strongly affected by the type of task in which participants engage. In a general knowledge quiz, participants laughed more in the cooperative setting, while during a poker chips game it was the competitive setting that elicited more laughter.

Future analyses of this dataset will focus on the mechanisms underlying these task-specific effects. One potential explanation of the present finding are the structural differences between the two games. The poker chips task was played during 2 minutes, and the general knowledge quiz lasted longer, up to approximately 15 minutes. In addition, since in the cooperative setting participants could discuss possible response options, quiz sessions tended to last longer than in the competitive setting. Although analyzing the number of laughs per minute controls for the differences in the duration of different games, it is possible that interactions between participants varied as a function of task duration. It is also worth noting that the poker chips task involved just the two participants of similar status, while the general knowledge quiz was led by the experimenter, thus being a 3-person interaction which could be marked by a different power dynamic. Finally, the general knowledge quiz would have been a familiar task to most participants; the poker chip task, on the other hand, would have been an unfamiliar task. The poker chip task required dyads to place a hand in a box of slime, with the potential for their hands to come into contact. It is possible that the higher occurrence of laughter in the competitive setting compared to the cooperative setting was a result of participants using laughter to mask any social awkwardness they were experiencing—this assumes greater levels of social awkwardness in competititve settings compared to cooperative settings. These proposed explanations for the observed interaction are, of course, speculative and will require further investigation.

The next steps of the present work will involve annotation and analysis of the amount of speech across the four games as a measure of participants' engagement. Examining laughter synchrony could provide further insights into how this signal contributes to building rapport and social cohesion. Overall, given that the mere frequency of laughter is a very general measure, pairing laughs with meaningful observable signals, such as speech, specific game events, or potentially even facial movements, could provide more specific insights into the meaning of laughter in different tasks and settings.

5. Bibliographical References

Barr, D., Levy, R., Scheepers, C., & Tily, H. (2013). Random effects structure for confirmatory hypothesis testing: Keep it maximal. *Journal of Memory And Language*, *68*(3), 255-278.

Bates, D., Mächler, M., Bolker, B., & Walker, S. (2015). Fitting linear mixed-effects models using lme4. *Journal of Statistical Software*, *67*(1), 1–48.

Bryant, G. A., Fessler, D. M. T., Fusaroli, R., Clint, E., Aarøe, L., Apicella, C. L., … Zhou, Y. (2016). Detecting affiliation in colaughter across 24 societies. *Proceedings of the National Academy of Sciences*, 113(17): 4682–4687.

Dunbar, R., Frangou, A., Grainger, F., & Pearce, E. (2021). Laughter influences social bonding but not prosocial generosity to friends and strangers. *PLOS ONE*, 16(8) : e0256229.

Kjeldgaard-Christiansen, J. (2018). Social signals and antisocial essences: The function of evil laughter in popular culture. *The Journal of Popular Culture*, 51(5): 1214-1233.

Magezi, D. A. (2015). Linear mixed-effects models for within-participant psychology experiments: An introductory tutorial and free, graphical user interface (LMMgui). *Frontiers in Psychology*, *6*, 2.

Martin, J., Rychlowska, M., Wood, A., & Niedenthal, P. (2017). Smiles as multipurpose social signals. *Trends In Cognitive Sciences*, *21*(11): 864–877.

McKeown, G., and Curran, W. (2015). "The relationship between laughter intensity and perceived humour," in *Proceedings of the 4th International Workshop on Laughter and Other Non-verbal Vocalisations in Speech*, eds K. Truong, D. Heylen, J. Trouvain, and N. Campbell (Dublin: Queen's University Belfast), 27–29.

Oveis, C., Spectre, A., Smith, P. K., Liu, M. Y., & Keltner, D. (2016). Laughter conveys status. *Journal of Experimental Social Psychology, 65*: 109–115.

Provine, R. (1993). Laughter Punctuates Speech: Linguistic, Social and Gender Contexts of Laughter. *Ethology*, 95(4): 291-298.

Vettin, J., & Todt, D. (2004). Laughter in conversation: Features of occurrence and acoustic structure. *Journal of Nonverbal Behavior*, *28*(2): 93–115.

Author Index